BFI Film Classics

The BFI Film Classics is a series of books that introduces, interprets and celebrates landmarks of world cinema. Each volume offers an argument for the film's 'classic' status, together with discussion of its production and reception history, its place within a genre or national cinema, an account of its technical and aesthetic importance, and in many cases, the author's personal response to the film.

For a full list of titles available in the series, please visit our website: <www.palgrave.com/bfi>

'Magnificently concentrated examples of flowing freeform critical poetry.'
Uncut

'A formidable body of work collectively generating some fascinating insights into the evolution of cinema.'
Times Higher Education Supplement

'The series is a landmark in film criticism.'
Quarterly Review of Film and Video

Night and the City

Andrew Pulver

A BFI book published by Palgrave Macmillan

First published in 2010 by
PALGRAVE MACMILLAN

on behalf of the

BRITISH FILM INSTITUTE
21 Stephen Street, London W1T 1LN
www.bfi.org.uk

There's more to discover about film and television through the BFI. Our world-renowned archive, cinemas, festivals, films, publications and learning resources are here to inspire you.

Palgrave Macmillan in the UK is an imprint of Macmillan Publishers Limited, registered in England, company number 785998, of Houndmills, Basingstoke, Hampshire RG21 6XS. Palgrave Macmillan in the US is a division of St Martin's Press LLC, 175 Fifth Avenue, New York, NY 10010. Palgrave Macmillan is the global academic imprint of the above companies and has companies and representatives throughout the world. Palgrave® and Macmillan® are registered trademarks in the United States, the United Kingdom, Europe and other countries.

Series cover design: Ashley Western
Series text design: ketchup/SE14
Images from *Night and the City*, © Twentieth Century-Fox Film Corporation

Set by Cambrian Typesetters, Camberley, Surrey
Printed in China

This book is printed on paper suitable for recycling and made from fully managed and sustained forest sources. Logging, pulping and manufacturing processes are expected to conform to the environmental regulations of the country of origin.

British Library Cataloguing-in-Publication Data
A catalogue record for this book is available from the British Library
A catalog record for this book is available from the Library of Congress
10 9 8 7 6 5 4 3 2 1
19 18 17 16 15 14 13 12 11 10

ISBN 978–1–84457–280–9

Contents

Acknowledgments

Grateful thanks to: James Hahn, Glenn Erickson, Rebecca Barden, Sophia Contento, Alistair Williams, Jill Reading, the BFI Stills Library, Leah Middleton, Lesley Thorne, Julian Grainger.

Introduction

It's the title that gets you first; somehow so elemental and sinewy. In four short words it yokes together two key twentieth-century fetishes: the black swamp of the night (with the moral terrors it summons up), and the newly concretised urban jungle, a man-made construction so elaborate that it appeared to have taken on a brutal life of its own. As a pairing, it is definitively modern and anti-pastoral. (No dappled greensward or lowing cattle here – they've been abolished). And with the careful positioning of a definite article, it becomes a phrase of pure, hard poetry of authentically modernist intent. Would *The Night and the City* have worked so well? Or *The Night and City*? Or even, God forbid, *City and the Night*? Not a chance.

The writer who came up with it, Gerald Kersh, attached it to his third novel. Published in 1938, *Night and the City* is a high-minded pulp thriller containing a fantastically vivid creation, Soho pimp (or ponce, as the term was then) Harry Fabian. A dapper dresser armed with a fake American accent, and a tenacious finagler in all corners of the petty-crime universe, Fabian is arguably the most finely drawn fictional example of the sharp-suited English hoodlum in the inter-war years. (The main rivals? Graham Greene's Pinkie in *Brighton Rock*, or maybe James Curtis's Kennedy in *The Gilt Kid*.) And though it's never fully spelled out in Kersh's effusive prose, Fabian is an ethnically radical character too: with a name like that, we know he's clearly supposed to be Jewish – a figure a long way from the earnest, poverty-stricken, fresh-off-the-boat characters in books like Israel Zangwill's *Children of the Ghetto*.

His implied ethnic background makes Fabian a figure to contend with, and potent icon at that. (A British Jewish gangster? We can't have enough of those.) There were plenty of real-life counterparts in the 1930s and 40s: street toughs like the Distelman brothers, Morris 'Moishe Blue Boy' Goldstein or Jack 'Spot' Comer. By the end of the decade, Comer could viably contend to be a major underworld figure as he 'took over' the West End[1] and carried out ethnically driven turf-war feuds with Italian roughnecks like Albert Dimes. Earlier, at the turn of the century, Whitechapel saw the gang know as the 'Bessarabian Tigers', led by Max Moses aka Kid McCoy.[2] From the 1880s onward, Soho had its own Jewish community, a necessary ingredient for any aspiring protection-racketeer, who needed solid ethnic turf to prey on. (I know this, if nothing else, because my grandfather, Alf Pulver, ran a tailor's workshop in Poland Street just after the war; his brother, Sid, commandeered a room for his unsuccessful bookie operation.)

Whatever the backdrop, that hook-em-in title would guarantee attention from the cinema world; more than anyone, a film producer would know its power. Kersh was fending off Hollywood even before his novel was published in the US. The film that eventually emerged –

set up by Darryl F. Zanuck at Twentieth Century-Fox, directed by McCarthy blacklistee Jules Dassin, led by Hollywood heavy Richard Widmark, shot in London – is like an island in the river of film noir. Not the least, because two distinct versions were completed: one for release in Britain and its empire, and one for the US and the rest of the world. Book and movie(s) don't bear a huge relation to each other, apart from Fabian and his predilection for bone-splintering wrestling promotions, but *Night and the City* is a kind of prism through which to look in a multitude of directions at once: at noir, at British pulp cinema, at communist crime novels, at Soho's own mythology.

It's fair to say that *Night and the City* has suffered a shifting reputation, even if film historians have maintained a consistent interest in it. In the wider world, of actual filmgoers and the media that interact with them, *Night and the City*'s stature has grown sharply in recent years. Here's an example: in 1981, the film's

Harry Fabian dodges the traffic in Upper St Martin's Lane

director Jules Dassin visited the National Film Theatre on London's South Bank for what was then called a Guardian Film Lecture, where his interlocutor was the late *Evening Standard* film critic Alexander Walker. The tape is in the British Film Institute's archive. Even though one of *Night and the City*'s key scenes was shot only yards away (in the Lambeth Lead Works' Shot Tower by the side of Waterloo Bridge, demolished in 1962), the film is not mentioned once in an hour-long discussion ranging over Dassin's entire career. You might argue that it is down to Walker's own prejudices, but no one in the audience asks him about it either – all they want to hear about is *Rififi* (1955) and his wife Melina Mercouri. In sharp contrast, twenty-one years later in 2002, *Night and the City* was celebrated with a centrepiece slot in the same venue at the Crime Scene film festival.

What had happened? The most dramatic change was the ascension of a new generation of cinematic taste-makers, led by the Coen brothers and Quentin Tarantino at the beginning of the 1990s –

Fabian on the run in Waterloo; the now-demolished Shot Tower looms in the background

a generation of taste-makers who prized pulp cinema (and novels) for their own sake. Both the Coens and Tarantino specialised in creating pastiche-oriented crime dramas that sparked scores of imitators, and simultaneously precipitated a shift in audience and critics' positions. In the UK, we had our own watered-down version of this, with the 1998 success of *Lock Stock and Two Smoking Barrels*, which triggered a nostalgic interest in key British crime cinema. *Lock Stock* is clearly much less astute about its forebears than *Reservoir Dogs* or *Miller's Crossing*, but we have to give it its due in popularising previously little-regarded areas of British crime cinema.

Night and the City has also benefited from another, largely independent school of critical thought, one that actually developed through interest in its original source material. Gerald Kersh's novel was a success in its day on both sides of the Atlantic, but it eventually joined other examples of 'lowlife' writing in bargain bins across the land. But urban archaeologists and psycho-geographers never lost sight of it, and in recent years *Night and the City* has joined a flotilla of defiantly indigenous novels – *The Gilt Kid*, *The Lowlife*, *Wide Boys Never Work*, *None but the Lonely Heart*, *The Crust on Its Uppers* – as a treasurable, and increasingly marketable, corner of the cult publishing world.

Kersh's current standing owes much to frequent mention in the work of Iain Sinclair (who contributed the foreword to London Books's recent reissue of *Wide Boys Never Work*). Sinclair's interest in east London novelists has led him naturally to Jewish writers like Alexander Baron (*The Lowlife*), Emanuel Litvinoff (*Journey through a Small Planet*) and Simon Blumenfeld (*Jew Boy*), and onwards towards Kersh. But Kersh is not of the school of Hackney and Bethnal Green; his *Night and the City* has little in common with other Jews' immigrant chronicles of rage and despair; it has much more affinity with the British pulp literature of the 1930s and 40s. Curtis, Richard Llewellyn, Graham Greene in his 'entertainment' phase, and Lawrence Meynell are Kersh's closest cousins in spirit, delineating as they do an argot-heavy world of petty crime, class conflict and bruising, street-smart morality. *Night and the City*'s chosen locale is Soho, in central London; the small district known for gang wars and the underground sex industry, the red-light activities that are the leading element in the squalid moral geometry that Kersh established in his novel. His protagonist, Harry Fabian, is a pre-war prototype of the post-war spiv – a wide boy and hoodlum always on the make – and Kersh's novel is a key entry in that most mythicised of London landscapes: brooding, nightmarish, infested Soho. As John King, author of *The Football Factory*, puts it in the foreword to a new edition of the novel:

Night and the City is set in the Soho of legend, itself a focus for the glitz of the West End. The book recreates a trail of pubs and clubs and Italian-run cafes from back in the days when a bowl of spaghetti was still exotic. Kersh knew this world and his sentences shine bright, his locations peopled by a nutty bunch of fluorescent characters with nuttier, more fluorescent names.[3]

Fabian on the run in the city; the dome of St Paul's framed in an archway

It is entirely fitting, then, that the film adaptation of Kersh's novel should go on to become a supreme example of London noir: nothing else really comes close. Its genesis, as we shall see, meant that it became the meeting point of distinct cinematic pathways: the American studio system, the ideological crisis of the McCarthy blacklist, the British pulp-thriller tradition in both book and film, the overarching influence of the wider film noir style. As a result, *Night and the City*'s is a cinematic hybrid of a quite exceptional nature: not only is it the product of international collaboration at a chaotic moment in cultural and creative history, but the same uncertainty resulted in a number of different edits of the film, two of which went on to dispute the status of 'official' version. It's almost as if the dodgy dealings and on-the-hoof spivvery of the narrative content somehow infected the activities of the film-makers themselves. Not for nothing does it deserve the label of 'spiv noir'. It's this process that this book is intended to trace: how *Night and the City* came together, splintered apart and was patched up again to become a bruised, limping, but indefatigable creation of post-war cinema.

1 The Film

Story

In the most familiar version of *Night and the City*, the film begins with a characteristically noir-ish voiceover, a 24-syllable line too lyrical not to be quoted in full:

Night and the city. The night is tonight, tomorrow night ... or any night. The city is London.

The suggestion is that director Jules Dassin himself spoke these lines, a move perhaps modelled on Carol Reed's opening lines for *The Third Man*, released in the UK while *Night and the City* was being shot. (Dassin is not credited, though, and another version – the 'British' one, which we will come to later – has a different voice.) His protagonist, Harry Fabian, first seen dashing past St Paul's Cathedral, is a man in a hurry – literally so, in the manner of Sammy Glick, the hero of Budd Schulberg's 1941 novel *What Makes Sammy Run?*. (Glick was the literary icon of American aspirationalism; Schulberg returned the compliment, unconsciously or not, by reproducing Fabian's line 'I just want to be somebody' in his celebrated script for *On the Waterfront*, 1954.)

Fabian is a Soho hoodlum, a ducker and diver, and the place he is dashing to is the walk-up flat belonging to his girl Mary. He's in need of money and is not above sneaking a look in her purse to see if there's any there. But Mary catches him in the act, and the pair clash over his endlessly elaborate schemes for raising cash – but in the end, she pops downstairs to her poloneck-jumpered neighbour Adam to borrow the fiver that will get Fabian off the hook.

Fabian then puts in an appearance at the Silver Fox nightclub, a hostess clip joint run by husband and wife team Phil and Helen

Nosseross, where he collects some more money. Next it's down to the Café Anglais 'American Bar' in Leicester Square, where he puts the moves on a trio of hapless American tourists. (His play is to pretend he's found a wallet – in reality his own – and then use the attempt to 'restore' it to its owner to recommend that the marks go to the Silver Fox.)

A couple of points: first, Fabian is American, like the actor portraying him, and there's no attempt to investigate or justify what an American is doing grubbing around Soho clubland. (The same is true of Mary and Adam.) Second, even though the most perfunctory analysis of the film would conclude that Fabian is a classic example of a post-war spiv, the word is not used anywhere in the script. Instead, Fabian is twice referred to as a 'tout'. This is surely due in part to the source material: Kersh's novel was written before the war when 'spiv' was not a widely used term. It is presumably also due to simple ignorance on the (American) scriptwriter Jo Eisinger's part.

Fabian struts confidently through Goodwin Court in Covent Garden, on his way to the Silver Fox nightclub

Fabian's fondness for the old wallet switcheroo affords him an unexpected opportunity in a wrestling hall. As he is thrown out for trying it on with the punters, he runs into retired wrestling legend Gregorius – who has just denounced fixed-bout grappling in front of his own son Kristo, a powerful hoodlum who has a lock on London's wrestling promotions. Sensing an opportunity, Fabian ingratiates himself with Gregorius, persuading the elderly fighter that he too has a yen for the purists' favourite, Greco-Roman wrestling. (Greco-Roman, an Olympic sport, only allows holds above the waist, and has never been associated with the tainted 'worked show' that still dominates professional catch wrestling.)

Fabian pitches his big idea to Phil Nosseross: a promotions outfit that Gregorius's participation means will be protected from Kristo. The Nosserosses ridicule his ambitions, and sneeringly promise to match his money if he can raise £200. Fabian tries all his shifty contacts – beggar 'king' Figler, the forger Googin, black

Inside the American Bar, Fabian lines up his marks

marketeer Anna O'Leary – but draws a blank until he is unexpectedly approached by Helen Nosseross herself, who, it turns out, has been nursing a secret yen for him. She has her own plan to ditch her husband and open her own club: she will use Fabian, she says, to get seed money from Phil. She gives Fabian the £200, in return for him getting the licence for her club. (Kristo and Nosseross, with their Greek-sounding names, are no doubt intended to evoke the Maltese element in the London underworld at the time, led by the Messina brothers who dominated the Soho vice racket during and after the war.)

But Fabian's plans unravel. One of Kristo's goons, the Strangler, picks a fight with Gregorius in Fabian's gym, even though he has been matched against Gregorius's protégé, Nikolas. After a violent physical confrontation, witnessed by Fabian as well as Kristo, Gregorius collapses and dies. Appalled by the death of his father, Kristo declares open season on Fabian, offering a thousand pounds to

Kristo comforts his dying father, Gregorius

the man who brings him in. Meanwhile, Helen realises Fabian has let her down, and sold her a fake licence. She returns to Phil, only to find that he has shot himself.

Fabian is forced to dash across London as he's pursued by the entire criminal fraternity ('the East End, Soho, the Embankment', in Kristo's words). He is eventually run to earth in Anna O'Leary's Chiswick boathouse. 'It's no good coming to me,' she says. 'I can't help you. Nobody can help you.' Fabian has no more running left in him – except when he's seized by a final inspiration to pay back his most significant debt. He tries to pass Mary off as the person who's fingered him to Kristo, so she can collect his thousand pounds. But Fabian is grabbed by the Strangler, who breaks his neck and throws the body in the river.

Production

On 5 July 1949, the *Daily Mail* reported that 'tomorrow' the American actor Richard Widmark would start work on a new film, called *Night and the City*. He was to be paid $400 per week (£100 at the time; some £7,600 in today's equivalent) and was given a flat in Mayfair and a cottage in the country. By his own admission, Widmark then spent '30 nights running around London'.[4] In fact, according to a Twentieth Century-Fox end-of-shoot press release issued in November 1949 as some of the principal cast embarked on the SS *American* for the homeward trip, *Night and the City* had shot for seventy-five days, of which Widmark had worked fifty-three, including twenty-seven nights.

The road to production was a typically tortuous one. Although Kersh's third novel was originally published in 1938, the war meant that America was deprived of it until 1946. Film producers were electrically attracted to what Tim Pulleine memorably calls its 'reverberant title'[5].

Paul Duncan, the foremost researcher on Kersh's life,[6] reveals in the audio commentary to the recently released DVD that agent-turned-producer Charles K. Feldman – who would soon go on to

make *The Glass Menagerie* (1950), *A Streetcar Named Desire* (1951) and *The Seven Year Itch* (1955) – paid Kersh $45,000 for the rights in 1946, and immediately set about putting it into production; and after going through a number of writers, he finally hired former police reporter Jo Eisinger to hammer out a script. Though largely forgotten now, Eisinger was a hot name in the mid-1940s, thanks to his credit for writing the screen adaptation of Columbia Studios' Rita Hayworth vehicle *Gilda* (1946), as well as authoring the mystery novel *The Walls Came Tumbling Down*, which was itself adapted into a Lee Bowman film for Columbia in 1946.

Despite attaching Jacques Tourneur – director of *Cat People* (1942) and *Out of the Past* (1947) among others – Feldman failed to get a production off the ground, and sold the rights (and script) on to Darryl F. Zanuck, the powerful vice-president of Twentieth Century-Fox. To get around British post-war currency regulations, Zanuck handed over production to Fox's UK office. The Anglo-American Film Agreement, negotiated by Board of Trade president Harold

Fabian embraces his doom, sprinting along the Thames embankment

Wilson in 1948, set a strict limit on the amount of money the US could take out of Britain in box-office receipts; the remainder had to be spent on production, rights and facilities in the UK.[7] (Protectionist as this may seem, it actually ended a boycott imposed by the Motion Picture Export Association of America [MPEA] after the Labour government imposed a 75 per cent import duty on films in 1947.)

This consideration for the UK film industry did not, however, extend to the principal figures assigned to make the film. Zanuck's pick to direct was Jules Dassin, who had run foul of the Hollywood blacklist as the House Un-American Activities Committee (HUAC) strengthened its grip on the film industry. Zanuck knew that Dassin, a Communist Party member until 1939, was about to be called to testify before the Committee, so dispatched him overseas out of their reach.[8] In Dassin's own words: 'Zanuck pushed this book in my hand, and said, you're leaving, you're getting out of here. You're going to London and you're going to make this, because this is probably the last picture you're ever going to make.' Dassin denied that he fled the US to escape testifying before HUAC:

As a matter of fact, when I was accused of being a subversive, I was abroad negotiating with the Italians to make a Fernandel film, *Il Camillo*. When I read about it, I went back to the US. I wanted to face the committee, but no one called me before it.[9]

However, *Night and the City* was the last film he would make for a Hollywood studio for almost fifteen years. After *Night and the City* was finished and released, Dassin's career was spectacularly crippled by the McCarthy witch-hunt, following testimony by fellow directors Edward Dmytryk and Frank Tuttle in 1951. Their identification of Dassin as a communist was enough to scupper any prospects of future employment. (Not surprisingly, many critics have subsequently seen *Night and the City* as channelling Dassin's own trauma of paranoia and flight.)

Dassin's early career revolved around radical theatre. He spent six years as part of a communist-inspired Yiddish troupe, Artef, in New York, under its legendary director Benno Schneider, an exile from the Zionist Habima theatre company in Moscow. ('We did *Sholem Aleicheim*. It had a political tint.'[10]) Dassin was radicalised by Clifford Odets's *Waiting for Lefty*, which he saw in 1935, and immediately joined the American Communist Party.[11] He also worked for the state-funded Federal Theater Project (set up by the New Deal agency Works Progress Administration), and the FTP's activities – such as the long-running Living Newspapers project, or the 1937 musical *The Cradle Will Rock* – were regularly accused of left-wing political bias. It was only after the FTP's funding was cancelled by its political enemies in Congress in 1939 that Dassin looked for work in the film industry. He was offered a contract with RKO, and became a 'watcher' – observing other directors at work. One of these was Alfred Hitchcock; Dassin 'watched' on *Mr and Mrs Smith* (1941). 'I was so intimidated by him. After every scene or take, he would turn around and yell, "Is that all right for you? May I print it?" '[12] RKO fired Dassin, but he found a job at MGM, who gave him his break, allowing him to direct a 20-minute adaptation of Poe's *The Tell-Tale Heart* (1941). He graduated to features with the wartime spy thriller *Nazi Agent* (1942) starring exiled actor Conrad Veidt, and was put to work in MGM's B department, resulting in a wide variety of work, including an adaptation of Oscar Wilde's *The Canterville Ghost* (1944) and the Lubitsch-esque romance *Two Smart People* (1946).

But Dassin fiercely resented the seven-year MGM contract, and ended up being fired again after a massive row with studio head, Louis B. Mayer. (Mayer reportedly yelled at him: 'Get out of here, you dirty Red!'[13]) Fortunately, he found work with independent producer Mark Hellinger – like Dassin, a left-leaning Jew schooled in New York radicalism – who hired him to make the Burt Lancaster prison pic *Brute Force* (1947). It was with this film that Dassin settled on the tough-nosed noir style that would make his name.

Hellinger was a former *New York Daily Mirror* syndicated columnist, and his Damon Runyon-esque sketches found a ready ear in Hollywood. One of his stories became the basis for the successful gangster film *The Roaring Twenties* (1939), and Hellinger headed for Hollywood to work for Warner Bros. He soon became fed up with studio strife, and made three great noirs as an independent producer: *The Killers* (1946), *Brute Force* and *The Naked City* (1948). Hellinger was initially reluctant to produce such a gritty, realism-orientated procedural, but was swayed by Dassin's enthusiasm. ('Are you out of your mind? It's a new genre, and we have to do it.'[14]) The resulting film was a seminal police thriller, openly inspired by the street crime photography of Weegee, and one that attempted to inject American cinema with the documentary techniques of Italian neo-realism; its impact was immediate. Hellinger, sadly, died before its release, though he did live long enough to record the film's opening narration: 'A city has many faces ... It's one o'clock in the morning now ... And this is the face of New York City ...'.

After Hellinger's death, Dassin returned to the studio system a hot directorial property and was hired by Twentieth Century-Fox to make another noir, *Thieves Highway* (1949). This starred Richard Conte, as a trucker out for revenge against a mobster who had crippled his father; it was made under the supervision of Darryl F. Zanuck, who would prove to be a key contact. As HUAC intensified its activities in regard to the entertainment industry during 1949, subpoenaing suspected communists, Zanuck took it upon himself to tip Dassin off and give him an excuse to leave the country. Dassin remembers that Zanuck gave him astute advice on the politics of getting the film finished: 'Get a screenplay out as fast as you can and start shooting the most expensive scenes. Then they might let you finish it.'[15]

Dassin left the US and headed for London to research locations with Eisinger. He later said that, though the film was repeatedly accused of inaccuracy by the British media, 'in actual fact ... I invented nothing, it was all there'.[16] His London fixer was Percy

Hoskins, who Dassin appeared to think was a Scotland Yard policeman; in fact, Hoskins was one of the best-known British crime reporters of the 1950s, chief crime correspondent of the *Daily Express* and later to become notorious for his questionable behaviour during the Dr John Bodkin Adams case. (Hoskins, alone among national newspaper crime correspondents, believed Adams not guilty of the murder of a number of his patients; after Adams was acquitted on a specimen murder charge in 1957, Hoskins paid him £10,000 for his life story and the pair became lifelong friends.) Hoskins would also become more intimately connected with the British film industry, as a number of his stories were turned into low-budget crime films – among them *The Blue Parrot* (1953) and *Dangerous Cargo* (1954).

Despite ongoing protests in Britain by the actors' union Equity at the importation of American performers, Zanuck installed Richard Widmark in the lead role, and, according to Dassin, asked for a minor character to be beefed up to provide Gene Tierney with a part. ('Zanuck called me, and said, you owe me one. I want you to cast Gene Tierney … she's just had a bad time, a very unhappy love affair and she's rather suicidal and she needs us to help.'[17]) Widmark, of course, had made his mark (and been nominated for an Academy Award) with his first significant screen role, that of cackling killer Tommy Udo in *Kiss of Death* (1947). A mild-mannered, milk-drinking Minnesotan, and a card-carrying political liberal, Widmark made for a reluctant noir villain, playing variations on the type in *The Street with No Name* (1948), *Road House* (1948) and *No Way Out* (1950) – in the last of which he played a rabidly racist bank robber whose target is Sidney Poitier, ironically a real-life friend. *Night and the City* sought, clearly, to exploit Widmark's notorious cackle, though it's more of a despairingly hysterical giggle than Udo's psychotically homicidal guffaw. Zanuck could hardly have made a better decision: as one critic later put it, Widmark is 'jumpy, erratic, damned … he adds a demonic rage to the role, his nervy hyped up acting perfectly matching Jules Dassin's powerful direction, which transforms elegant London into a city of fear'.[18]

Gene Tierney, on the other hand, was a fully established Hollywood star, having been signed by Zanuck in 1940, and cast in a string of hit movies. An Oscar nomination came for *Leave Her to Heaven* (1945), in which she played Cornel Wilde's pyschopathic wife; the popular hit *The Ghost and Mrs Muir* (1947) had her communing with an apparition played by Rex Harrison; but her defining role, however, is without doubt the Otto Preminger-directed noir *Laura* (1944), in which she plays the (dead) woman with whom detective Dana Andrews (and newspaperman Clifton Webb) is obsessed. Tierney's strength as a performer was always an underlying sense of emotional fragility – which appeared to be confirmed off screen when she entered a psychiatric hospital in 1954 and essentially disappeared from acting for the rest of the decade. In retrospect, the troubles that Dassin alluded to above fed into her tightly wound on-screen persona in *Night and the City*, and was something she was unable to escape in the years ahead. Unfortunately, her main showstopper in *Night and the City* – the red dress she wears in the

A study in opposites: Fabian broods, Mary reminisces

Silver Fox – is denied us by the black-and-white cinematography; an image of it survives in a colour production still.

But Dassin did use locals for the less prominent roles; though, as he admits, he had to rely on Douglas Fairbanks Jr, who worked for Fox in London. 'Most of the casting was not my doing at all; I didn't know the London scene. Fairbanks … did most of the casting for me.'[19] Francis L. Sullivan, who alternated stage roles with small but striking film performances (he played, for example, Mr Bumble in Lean's *Oliver Twist*, 1949), was hired as club owner Nosseross, his devious wife Helen was played by Googie Withers, and Herbert Lom, later to play a not dissimilar role in a comedic context in *The Ladykillers* (1955), came aboard as the local hoodlum Kristo. Of this key British-based trio, Withers was by some distance the most significant: she had already played major roles for Ealing in the chiller compendium *Dead of Night* (1945), where she plays the girl in the haunted-mirror segment; *Pink String and Sealing Wax* (1945) as a homicidal wife of a Brighton pub landlord; and *It Always Rains on Sunday* (1947), a nuanced and sensitive study of difficult post-war times in the East End of London. She was much courted by Hollywood,[20] and was approached by Fox as a last-minute replacement for *Night and the City* after Merle Oberon dropped out shortly before filming started. (Oberon was otherwise occupied with her attempt to divorce her husband Lucien Ballard and marry her Italian lover Count Giorgio Cini.) Lom, on the other hand, was a émigré from Prague who had come to Britain in 1939, and whose work in films like *Young Mr Pitt* (1942) had led to a contract offer from Fox – which he was unable to take up after being denied a visa.[21] Still, Fox were able to offer him the role of Kristo, where his accented English was an asset.

Further down the cast list, there were bit parts for Kay Kendall (later to marry Rex Harrison and die tragically young of leukaemia), *Carry On* stalwart Peter Butterworth and James Hayter (known for his Mr Kipling TV voiceovers).

But Dassin's most spectacular casting coup was for the role of Kristo's father, the veteran wrestler known as Gregorius the Great.

Dassin reported later how Zanuck had insisted that he simply hire a beefy actor.[22] Dassin held out for a dimly remembered figure from his childhood – a wrestler of near-mythical status named Stanislaus Zbyszko. Dassin may not have known it at the time, but along with the likes of Frank Gotch, Georg Hackenschmidt and 'The Great Gama', Zbyszko helped to create the first golden age of professional wrestling in the US and Europe. In wrestling, it was an advantage to have an East European or Asian cachet, so Zbyszko had little need to disguise his Polish origins. Though Zbyszko was able to fully claim a world title only in 1925, shortly before he retired, he excelled at both the purist Greco-Roman style and the more rough-and-tumble 'catch' grappling that achieved much greater worldwide popularity, and became the basis for the 'worked' bout that has since become the wrestling norm. By the late 1940s, Zbyszko had completely dropped off the radar, but a sports reporter friend of Dassin's tracked him down to a chicken farm in New Jersey. Dassin took a chance on him as Gregorius, and grew to

Gregorius and the Strangler go at it in Fabian's gym

admire him ('a very cultured gent, spoke many languages ... and of all the people on the film, if I went to an experimental theatre, he's the man that would come with me'[23]). Zbyszko wasn't the only pro wrestler on set: though much less successful in the ring, Mike Mazurki was hired to play the Strangler (the man who eventually kills Fabian). Mazurki, however, had already established himself as an actor after occupying the lower reaches of fight bills, playing Moose Malloy in *Murder My Sweet* (1944). Dassin knew Mazurki from casting him in a small role in *The Canterville Ghost* in the same year.

Filming began in July 1949, with cinematographer Max Greene behind the camera. Before the war, Greene had been known as Mutz Greenbaum; the Berlin-born cameraman had worked on scores of German silents through the 1920s – including *Die Försterchristel* (1926), *Der goldene Abgrund* (1927), *Liebeshölle* (1928) and *Sensation im Wintergarten* (1929) – before emigrating to Britain in 1931. Greenbaum flourished in the UK, working on high-profile films from the beginning. His first UK credit of consequence was *Hindle Wakes* (1931), the Victor Saville-directed study of working-class holiday-making. During the war, Greenbaum mutated into Greene and Mutz to Max, a not-uncommon act of attention-deflecting assimilation. As Greene, he continued to do well, shooting the astonishingly popular light-comedy series with Anna Neagle and Michael Wilding; these included *Piccadilly Incident* (1946), *The Courtneys of Curzon Street* (1947) and – biggest of all – *Spring in Park Lane* (1948). *Night and the City*, with its dramatic chiaroscuro and head-cracking violence, was a real change of pace, but Greene already had experience of filming seedy British crime stories, in the shape of *The Green Cockatoo* (1937) and *There Ain't No Justice* (1939). The former, written by Graham Greene, and the latter by James Curtis, count as dress rehearsals for *Night and the City*, even if neither, plain as they are visually, showcases the cinematographer's art to the same extent.

After *The Naked City*, Dassin knew that street shooting was his major strength, and his trips with Hoskins resulted in a number of

authentic-smell locations. The exterior of Mary's flat is proper Soho:
Richmond Buildings, an alleyway off Dean Street. (The building is no
longer there – replaced by a modern office block – and the street itself
now acts as the entranceway to a large hotel.) The doorway and
stairwell of the Silver Fox nightclub is in Goodwin's Court, running
between St Martin's Lane and Bedfordbury, then a pretty grubby part
of the West End, now a spring-cleaned offshoot of Covent Garden.
The bar where Harry puts the make on the American tourists was in
Leicester Square, where Harry Roy was the resident bandleader in
1949. (Incredibly, a taxi can stop right outside. And in the back of

Cinematographer Max Greene (left) and director Jules Dassin do their stuff

one shot, you can see hundreds of people lining the pavement to watch the film crew in action.) The King's Hall in Elephant and Castle is the fight venue used for the scenes where Fabian weasels his way into Gregorius's favour. And in the final chase sequence, Fabian staggers across the rubble of the South Bank, then being rebuilt for the Festival of Britain, with a recently completed Waterloo Bridge clearly visible in the background. The interiors, on the other hand, were largely studio sets, more in keeping with the conventional industry practice of the time.

If Dassin's priority was to find ultra-authentic locations, the film's camerawork is an intriguing mix of carefully calibrated noir style and freewheeling documentary-style coverage. The former is exemplified by the high-noir sequences in the Shot Tower as the film approaches its climax: Fabian is being stalked by Kristo's knifeman and Greene lets loose a full battery of expressive technique – shadows, silhouettes, vertiginous perspectives, skewed camera angles. The latter, on the other hand, is showcased in a particularly

A taxi pulls up on the east side of Leicester Square. No longer a possibility

memorable shot with a fixed camera in the back of a car, à la Joseph H. Lewis's *Gun Crazy* (1950), as one of Kristo's hoodlums speeds through Piccadilly Circus spreading the word to get Fabian. Dassin also favoured using multiple camera set-ups for extended sequences, such as the opening sprint across the steps of St Paul's Cathedral, to avoid any unnecessary break in the action and to get things done quickly. It also, of course, serves the vérité style. The technique came into its own for the climactic final scene, when Fabian runs along the riverside and is thrown, dead, from Hammersmith Bridge. The script called for it to happen at dawn, which meant that there was only a tiny window with the correct light. Dassin opted to use six cameras running in sequence to film Widmark's performance, moving lights and relocating cameras where necessary. It was all done in two days. He said later: 'We rehearsed it and that whole thing is take one, from one camera to another. That was quite a day.'[24]

Filming finished in November 1949, and the film was ready for theatrical release by the middle of the following year. In the intervening period, two different edits were made, one British and one American, with different scores. (The British had music by Benjamin Frankel, the American by Franz Waxman.) Dassin says he had no knowledge of a second edit[25] – i.e. 'the British' one – though being blacklisted, he was kept out of the cutting room while Fox were putting the film together, and only had telephone contact with the studio's editors. (He remained somewhat bitter about the fact that no face-to-face meeting, away from the studio lot, was ever suggested by the editing team. 'We were avoided like the plague,' he said.[26]) It is the 'American' version that has survived, and was officially endorsed by Dassin before his death in 2008.

Adaptation
Inevitably, there are several layers of archaeology to expose in *Night and the City*. The first, of course, is the relationship between the film and the original source novel. Kersh's disdain for the screen

adaptation was already well known: a Reuters news report from September 1949, during the film's production, was the first airing of his much-repeated sneer that he had been paid £10,937 per word, for four words: the title. Dassin was to confess that he had not read the novel before shooting:

I only read it much much later, because there was no time. We had to get the script going, and I was under this pressure. It was Bruce Goldstein [director of repertory programming for New York art cinema, Film Forum] who finally sent it to me – and it was a whole other story! When I was in London, they asked me: did you know how angry Gerald Kersh was with the film? I said – well, I'm sure he's right, as I never read it.[27]

Was Kersh right to be annoyed? Yes and no. Yes, because Dassin's film – aside from the names, lowlife setting and general milieu – bears little resemblance to his work, and no writer likes to see their masterpiece trashed; and no, because the success of the film has contributed considerably to the book's longevity – *Night and the City* has survived while most of Kersh's other works have disappeared into literary oblivion.

So what, if anything, survived the wreckage of the Feldman/Zanuck treatment? Like the film Fabian, Kersh's original is always on the hunt for a few bob; but he is explicitly identified as a 'ponce' – or 'Johnny Ronce', in rhyming slang – rather than a 'tout'. (This is 'ponce' in the now somewhat outdated sense of what we'd call a pimp; in the novel, Fabian principally lives off the 'immoral earnings' of his streetwalker girlfriend, Zoe.) Kersh's Fabian habitually pretends to be American (ostentatiously using transatlantic slang), and has his own scheme for getting into wrestling promotion, but also has other, nastier sidelines, like blackmailing hapless clients of Zoe. (That's how he funds his stake in the wrestling promotion business.) In the novel, Figler isn't a Dickensian type beggar-king; he's a small-time wheeler-and-dealer whom Fabian tries to make his partner in Fabian Promotions. Fabian's connection with the Silver

Fox is only that of a customer; it's there he runs into Helen, who is one of the showgirls, and not Nosseross's wife (who is in fact called Mary). It's Helen who is involved with Adam the sculptor; Adam, however, rejects his artistic poverty and is first taken on as a waiter by the Silver Fox, then becomes a wrestler himself. Ambitious Helen makes a move for the apparently well-off Fabian, who then tries to palm Zoe off on what was once called a 'white slaver', but is now called a sex trafficker. Fabian's first promotion ends in disaster when his star wrestler, a veteran called Ali the Terrible Turk, dies in his dressing room. Adam (clearly a fictional counterpart to Kersh himself) decides to quit the lowlife to return to his art. Annoyed over Fabian's repeated (broken) promises to buy him a silk dressing gown, another wrestler, called the Strangler, is out for Fabian's blood. But before the Strangler can get to him, Fabian is arrested as part of a pre-Coronation clean-up. (This means that the novel's action is dated to early 1937.)

Even in this brief summary, it's clear that many elements of the original reappear in the film, only reshuffled and reconfigured. Fabian no longer pretends to be American, he *is* American. The film's Helen is a conflation of two of the novel's women: Nosseross's unfaithful wife and the ambitious showgirl who tries to use Fabian to get ahead in the club world. (She also gets to use some of Kersh's most memorable material: namely, the lecture Nosseross gives to the aspiring club hostess on how to take the most money off the mugs, including mark-ups on cigarettes, cocktails, chocolates and breakfast food.) Apart from being Fabian's girl, the film Mary has little in common with the novel's Zoe.

In accordance with the requirements of 1940s thriller cinema, the film-makers have extracted a focused and honed narrative from Kersh's sprawling picaresque. Their most significant invention is Kristo, the gangland boss whom Fabian attempts to take on. (In the novel, the main physical threat comes from the buffoonish figure of the Strangler – converted to a figure of real menace in the film.) The post-fight death of the old-timer becomes the film's pivotal event;

and the film-makers engineer a climax, with Fabian running for his life across London, that is, again, entirely their own invention. It's clear that they felt compelled to add generic plot triggers to reconfigure Fabian as a doomed figure who is a co-conspirator in his own downfall; a key noir theme. Hence, the script calls for a father–son bond (between Kristo and Gregorius) that is shown to be stronger than mere avarice, and will be a deadly weapon of vengeance when it is disrupted. It is Fabian's recognition of his own impending demise, and his creative money-raising approach to it, that puts *Night and the City* into the same knows-it's-coming category as *Double Indemnity* (1944), *D.O.A.* (1950) and *Le Jour se lève* (1939).

This all feeds into a reshaped conception of Fabian's character. In Kersh's novel, Fabian is a dapper, unsentimental showboater, rarely venturing outside the square mile of Soho and the West End, unreflective and ungrateful. The film Fabian, on the other hand, is constantly in mental and emotional turmoil, desperate to prove himself at every turn … and sweating, always sweating. His end, when it comes, is that of a cornered animal; blinded by the glare of the headlights, as it were. He is even given a cursory backstory; Mary shows him a photo of the pair of them in younger days: 'Remember them, Harry? Nice people. Nice to know and be with. Remember the plans they used to make? The kind of life they were going to live?' And at the death, there's a passing reference to some early life agonies: 'All my life I've been running. From welfare officers … thugs … my father.' It's hardly a convincing attempt to establish a proper psychological context, but you have to give them points for trying.

The 'British version'

Because of its transatlantic production background, it isn't all that surprising that two different release versions of the film exist. A 101-minute edit was made for the audience in Britain and its 'dominions', and 96-minute cut prepared for the US. The opening credits suggest that the British edit was made first: for the British version, the editor is named as Sidney Stone; but by the time the American print was finished, Stone is jointly credited with Nick De Maggio, a Hollywood veteran who had worked for Dassin before on *Thieves Highway*. As mentioned before, it's the American edit that has become the standard, with Dassin apparently unaware that a British cut existed at all. Fortunately, the British Film Institute's National Film Archive holds a restored copy of it.

So how do the two films differ? First, and most obviously, they each have their own score. The British version has music by Benjamin Frankel; a prolific musical director before the war, Frankel became increasingly concerned with serious classical composition after it, remaining best known perhaps for his 1951 Violin Concerto 'To the Memory of the Six Million'. Frankel, the son of Jewish immigrants to Britain, was also ironically enough a Communist Party member at the time of *Night and the City*. The man behind the American score, on the other hand, was Franz Waxman. Waxman was also the scion of an émigré Jewish family, but he was born in Germany and won his first significant film-score assignments for high-profile German directors like Robert Siodmak on *Der Mann, der seinen Mörder sucht* (1931) and Fritz Lang on *Liliom* (1934). After leaving for the US in 1934, Waxman began a distinguished Hollywood career with James Whale's *Bride of Frankenstein* (1935), reunited with Lang on *Fury* (1936) and thereafter worked at the top end of the industry until the 1960s, creating music for Hitchcock (*Rebecca*, 1940, *Suspicion*, 1941, *Rear Window*, 1954), Billy Wilder (*Sunset Blvd*, 1950, *The Spirit of St Louis*, 1957) and Howard Hawks (*Air Force*, 1943).

Musicologist Christopher Husted, who compiled the notes for the SAE-CRS release of both scores, writes that Frankel signed his contract in January 1950, and in March of that year the Royal Philharmonic were engaged to perform his music. In the intervening period, however, a cable arrived at Twentieth Century-Fox's London outpost from head office with specific orders, as Husted quotes:

'For various reasons we deem it necessary to rescore and rerecord substantial parts if not all of *Night and the City* for American market.'[28] In mid-February, Waxman was hired to write a score in Hollywood.

No one knows for sure what motivated this decision; the most conventional explanation is that the American market had different demands from the British. James Hahn, Nitrate Film Curator at the AMPAS Film Archive, recently unearthed a third version, never released, of *Night and the City*; running at 111 minutes, it is assembled from both US and UK versions, using the longest sequences from each, and has Frankel's score attached. This would appear to support the idea that an early assembly was being looked at in head office, using the first (British) cut as the base. Husted also suggests that contractual differences between American and British composers may have played a part. Frankel's contract allowed him ownership of the music he composed, and therefore limited how far the studio could exploit it. Hollywood contracts were very different; the studios owned the music. It was very much in Fox's interests to supplant the British score with an American one, thus guaranteeing receipt of all performance and copyright earnings.

In terms of their musical impact, it's clear straight away that Frankel's vision is considerably more modest and restrained than Waxman's. Or, looking at it the other way, as Husted puts it: 'Waxman clearly had a much darker and bitter reaction to the film than Frankel did.'[29] The difference in approach is immediately obvious in the opening scene, as Fabian dashes across the front of St Paul's. In the British version, Frankel opts for a melodic, almost wistful accompaniment, while Waxman goes for bombastic neurosis par excellence. It's perhaps not a surprise that the more experienced scorer goes confidently for a fuller, more expressive sound, and there's no doubt that Waxman's music appears to amplify Fabian's own troubles to suitably hysterical levels.

But something interesting happens in the parallel chase scene that occurs close to the end of the film, when Fabian is again running for his life through the rubble under Waterloo Bridge. While Waxman once again goes for full-throated panic-attack music, Frankel barely includes any accompaniment, and instead allows the industrial sounds of diggers, pumps and drills to come through loud and clear.

Some interpretations would see this as a weakness, and a missed opportunity (and no doubt head office preferred Waxman's more obviously excitable treatment). But what's rather impressive about this scene in the British edit is that the atmospheric sound has its own particular effect, locking the drama into a physical space and making it bruisingly authentic. Waxman's music may play muscularly on the emotions, but it also has the effect of enclosing the drama in a hermetic bubble. Frankel's approach makes it seem, for want of a better word, more real. We can extrapolate the priorities and strengths of the two different approaches: Waxman/Hollywood have only a superficial sense of *Night and the City*'s physical space, and therefore reduce its importance as their generic techniques create a robust, fiction-centred entertainment; while Frankel/Britain, you sense, have an affinity with the detail of urban landscape, and have no problem allowing it to seep into the experience of the film. The fleetingly glimpsed buildings and streets in the background of a film can play a part, if you let them.

The same, interestingly, is true of the opening voiceover. In the British print, a British voice speaks the same words, but his tone is more matter of fact and less self-consciously lyrical than the American one. It's almost as if a local is unable to rhapsodise about the post-war London rubble and its doom-haunted streets; only an outsider, one infected with the myth-making, romanticising habits of American cinema, can take the poetic view. If *Night and the City* is a uniquely mid-Atlantic construction, it's here we can see an aesthetic fault-line developing. The British instinct is for low-key; the American for high.

All this is borne out by more detailed comparison of the two versions, for which we must again thank James Hahn. What has emerged from his shot-by-shot comparison is that the American re-edit – some 5 minutes shorter – is not simply the result of snipping out a few scenes. The US version includes some scenes that do not appear in the British version, while others are used at a more extended length; and in some instances, different dialogue sequences carved from the same general scene are used. The most obvious example of this latter practice is one of the early scenes, when Fabian fetches up in Mary's flat having escaped the two goons chasing him around St Paul's. In the British edit, Fabian tries to talk Mary into giving him money for one of his apparently inexhaustible supply of get-rich-quick schemes – the 'Fabian fuel pill' which he has lifted from 'Little Alf', a Whitechapel chemist. The 'Fabian fuel pill', it turns out, is designed to be added to a car's petrol tank to increase its mileage (though quite how it works if you need to set light to it is never fully explained). In the now-familiar sequence from the American edit, he enters Mary's dark and deserted flat, and is about to take cash out of her handbag when she interrupts him; he then attempts to wheedle money out of her to invest in a greyhound track in Birmingham. Fabian, here, comes off as considerably more sneaky and exploitative. The scene subsequently plays out on a similar trajectory in both prints, with Mary refusing to help and brandishing a photograph of their younger days (a different one in the US and UK versions) and Fabian responding: 'I just want to be somebody'. But the American version has entirely different blocking and actor movements, suggesting that a reshoot was ordered. (Perhaps Zanuck felt the first attempt, probably the one that ended up in the British version, was too sulky and wheedling to hold an American audience. Paul Duncan, in his audio commentary to the DVD, suggests that Zanuck himself may have directed a reshoot.)

A not-dissimilar effect was engineered by a change in a later scene, the Nosseross-kiss sequence (which apparently so disgusted Googie Withers, off screen as well as on). The first half of the scene in the British version – another wheedling section of dialogue, in which Helen tries to pocket some of the money Phil is counting at his

desk – is cut entirely, leaving the American edit to start at the point
where Helen is trying on the fox fur Phil gives her. The American
version can therefore focus on the unwanted kiss, and Phil's bizarre,
fetishist snuffling over the fur that finishes the sequence.
Deviance was very much part of the American noir arsenal;
no wonder Zanuck liked this bit.

 The most telling change occurs in the very last frames of the
film. In the final scene, as it played out for American audiences,
the Strangler dumps Fabian's body in the Thames, and Kristo flicks a
casual cigarette in after him. That's it, the end. This is as bleak and
nasty a finish as film noir ever saw. A human being reduced to a fag-
end. The British version, in contrast, is locked into the convention of
the young-lovers happy ending. The choreography of character
entrance and exit is reordered in the editing room so that, *after*
Fabian is killed, Adam the sculptor races over to comfort Mary, and
the pair walk over Hammersmith Bridge as the dawn light floods the

Phil Nosseross drapes a fur around the shoulders of his reluctant wife

sky. Not only does this provide a happy, upbeat ending in total contrast to the American edit, it also wraps up with some neatness the diurnal structure evoked by the title. The night, it seems, is over – along with Harry Fabian.

Other, smaller, adjustments are made throughout, which provide only minor amplifications of plot and motive. The British version, for example, contains scenes in which Phil Nosseross witnesses a kiss between Fabian and Helen outside his window (thereby making him slightly less of a deluded cuckold), and Mary and Adam work out that Fabian is in lethal trouble when Kristo's lawyer, Chilk, and his heavy, Yosh, interrupt their dinner – explaining the otherwise gaping plot hole as to how they even know to look for a panicking Fabian in the final scene. Then there are the weird little details that were presumably changed to ease the film past the US audience: a strange cutaway with a dwarf doorman shouting at Fabian is lost from the British edit, as is a nice shot of Fabian

Kristo gets ready to stub out his cigarette – and Fabian's life – from Hammersmith Bridge swinging onto the back of a United Dairies truck as he heads downriver from Waterloo. (It would have been lost on Americans that Hammersmith Bridge is several miles from the Shot Tower.)

Glenn Erickson, film critic and reviewer on the DVD Savant website, tells a story of buying a Twentieth Century-Fox original script of the film in 1976, and finding Darryl Zanuck's handwritten annotations inside.[30] He ascertained that Zanuck removed the original 'soft' introductory scenes 'in which [Fabian] did magic tricks and played the wistful dreamer', and describes a deleted scene in which Fabian hides 'in a bombed out church, whose senile former sexton thinks Harry is a burglar come to steal the long absent holy artifacts. In his pathetic state of denial, the sexton believes his church to be intact and functioning in this godless city.'[31] Whatever the film may have lost or gained thematically by its deletion, this scene appears to be the narrative's most explicit connection with the wartime assault on London; elsewhere, the rubble of the Blitz is confined to an atmospheric backdrop. It seems that *Night and the City* would not be allowed to be shackled too closely to a time and place.

The reviews

The first British film reviewers really put the boot in. Their principal complaint was exactly that which Zanuck had spent much time on eradicating: it all seemed very inauthentic. The *Monthly Film Bulletin* called *Night and the City* 'a violent and somewhat unrealistic story ... the crooks are never exactly placed: the Soho atmosphere is quite missing ... serious faults in a film which depends on the realism of the setting. Dassin remains a tourist in London.'[32] In *The Sunday Times*, Dilys Powell went much further, sneering at the film's ersatz nature.[33] She sees 'London's landmarks, but certainly not London ... a never-never city that does service in the cinema for any capital'. Having commended the 'British' cinematography (ironically, the work of German émigré Max Greene), Powell continues:

Except for its camera-work it is squalid and brutish … One stretches with relief when Mr Widmark, having trotted non-stop from Waterloo to Hammersmith … allows himself to be dropped in the Thames. *Night and the City* will presumably pass for a British film. It is about as British as *Sing Sing* and will do the British cinema nothing but harm.

Ouch.

Other critics concurred. The *Sunday Pictorial* called it 'a cheap, tawdry gangster melodrama set against a pretty incredible London',[34] and the *Star* got in with a cheap patriotic shot: 'The backgrounds are there, but the real flavour of London is missing. You have only to compare *Night and the City* with our own *The Blue Lamp* to see that.'[35] The only reasonably positive response I could find was from the *News of the World*'s Ewart Hodgson: 'While I hope *Night and the City* is a libel on the London underworld and suffers from being overdrawn and grossly larger than life, it has much merit as entertainment, particularly for those who like their screen fare speedily paced and sinewy.'[36]

The Blue Lamp (1950) comparison is telling. The fear that British cinema might be overwhelmed by a Hollywood invasion was a live one in the immediate post-war period (hence Harold Wilson's Anglo-American Film Agreement, mentioned above). In her review, Powell voices her scepticism that Hollywood could be trusted, repeating an anonymous director's assertion that they would 'move in with Hollywood script, Hollywood director, and a largely Hollywood cast'.[37] Modern critics Steve Chibnall and Robert Murphy concur, asserting that along with the James Hadley Chase adaptation *No Orchids for Miss Blandish* (1948), '*Night and the City* was treated with such hostility because [it] was seen as a Hollywood incursion'.[38] *The Blue Lamp*, along with *Brighton Rock* (1947), *They Made Me a Fugitive* (1947) and a handful of others, allowed crime cinema to assert a British national identity. Critic Tim Pulleine theorises that *Night and the City* is 'an act of reclamation … Hollywood renewing its title on generic properties that have been at risk of partial appropriation by British producers'.[39] While it's difficult to see Zanuck genuinely terrified at the prospect of Richard Attenborough or Trevor Howard making any kind of dent in America's pre-eminence as purveyors of hard-boiled crime cinema, the point is well made: battered and rubble-strewn London was more than just a convenient place to distribute otherwise frozen production finance. It was a landscape ripe for investing with the tortured motifs of film noir. It was all laid out for them.

How did American critics respond when the film was released in the US? Bosley Crowther, *The New York Times*'s legendary miserablist, offered nothing but contempt: 'It is little more than a melange of maggoty episodes having to do with the devious endeavors of a cheap London night-club tout to corner the wrestling racket – an ambition in which he fails.'[40] One the other hand, *Variety* gave it a major thumbs up: 'An exciting, suspenseful melodrama … the story of a double-crossing heel who finally gets his just desserts [*sic*].'[41] Despite the blacklist, Dassin is named and gets full credit: 'Jules Dassin, in his direction, manages extraordinarily interesting backgrounds, realistically filmed to create a feeling both of suspense and mounting menace.'[42]

It's possible to surmise that *Variety* was responding to the highly charged craftsmanship on show, with a Hollywood-ish lack of concern for specifics. We can see here confirmed the basic divergence between the British and American critical approaches to the film right from the start: the British primarily concerned with its authenticity (or lack of it), and the US appreciation of it as an exercise in noir style. In fact, the American view of the film is very much tempered by its visual stylings. With huge numbers of noirs to dissect and analyse, American critics could consider *Night and the City*'s narrative content a little rudimentary compared to the psychosexual masterworks inspired by James M. Cain or Dorothy B. Hughes; but it was its visual style that made it attention-grabbing. In their influential 1974 picture essay, Place and Peterson have no hesitation in including the film alongside such key noirs as *The Big Heat* (1953), *Double Indemnity*, *In a Lonely*

Place (1950) and *They Live by Night* (1948) as an exemplar of sinister lighting and dehumanising frame composition.[43] (The two shots they pick are a creepy close-up of Phil Nosseross with 'unusual shadows'[44] on his face; and Fabian filmed from inside a stairwell, his smallness in the frame emphasised by 'bold architectural lines'[45].)

There is also a third strand of critical input into *Night and the City*: the French. The film was released in France in December 1950, cementing Dassin's position among French critics as a director to watch following the 1948 release of *The Naked City*. Georges Sadoul regarded the earlier film as 'a candid, real and unadorned view of the bared face of a city',[46] and the later one as 'a sharp, violent and explosive film'.[47] François Truffaut, writing a few years later for *Arts* magazine, explained that 'from *Naked City* on, every new "Dassin" was awaited impatiently, and this waiting period was always rewarded'.[48] He particularly admired *The Naked City*'s 'documentary' style, a non-intrusive technique he later observed for himself while watching Dassin film an 'amazing' scene for *Rififi* in the Port Royal metro station. (*Rififi* would go to Cannes in 1955, where Dassin won the Best Director award jointly with Sergei Vasilyev for *Heroes of Shipka*.) Truffaut considered that *Night and the City* possessed 'a true epic inspiration' and called it 'definitely the best of Dassin's films',[49] even if it had not performed so well at the box office. French critics, especially the more radical ones, presumably empathised with Dassin's troubles with the blacklist (Sadoul mentions it repeatedly), and it naturally came up in what in retrospect looks like one of cinema's all-time great encounters, when Truffaut and Claude Chabrol interviewed Dassin for the April 1955 issue of *Cahiers du cinéma*. They told Dassin that, of all his films, *Night and the City* was the one they liked best ('C'est le film de vous que nous préférons'[50]). As well as their admiring comments about Widmark's performance, the 'très grande poésie' that is the shock ending and the Hugh Marlowe spaghetti scene, an idiosyncratic picture caption – 'Har-ry Fabian-se-ra-bien-tôt-le-promoteur-ex-clu-sif-de-la-lutte-gréco-ro-maine-à-Londres. Bing!'[51] – shows they were

particularly drawn to the off-the-cuff scene where Widmark pats out
his excitement on the Silver Fox's drum kit. Given the Nouvelle
Vague's later appetite for freewheeling improvisation and studiously
chaotic *mise en scène*, it's revealing that they zeroed in on this
unmistakable Widmark ad lib.

However, it's fair to say that *Rififi* firmly eclipsed *Night and the
City* in French minds; the sight of an American gangster-film director
filming right on their patch in Paris to such brilliant effect focused the
French critics' minds wonderfully. In Truffaut's view, Dassin 'reveals
Paris to us Frenchmen as he revealed London to the English (*Night
and the City*) and New York to the Americans (*The Naked City*)'.[52]
Even if he somewhat misjudged the extent to which the 'English' felt
London had been revealed to them by *Night and the City*, Truffaut
seems to have swiftly moved on from it, declaring *Rififi* 'the best
crime film I have ever seen' in his review for *Arts*.[53] If nothing else,
Rififi appeared to confirm for Truffaut the efficacy of the auteur
theory: considering the 'modest' budget and unremarkable source

'Sitt-ing-at-my-desk': the Fabian drum solo that so tickled Truffaut and Chabrol

material, it demonstrated to him 'that a film's success depends more on its director than on massive production resources or the participation of world renowned actors'.[54]

But before *Rififi*-mania could completely take hold, Raymond Borde and Etienne Chaumeton, in *Panorama du film noir américain* (1941–53) – the first full-length attempt to define noir, published in 1955 – gave *Night and the City* a central place in their study by using, on its cover, a photograph of Widmark's frantic, haunted face, cradling a lit match in his cupped hand. (When the book was translated into English in 2002, this image was replaced by a still from the somewhat more conventionally iconic *The Postman Always Rings Twice*, 1946.) For Borde and Chaumeton, the films they were struggling to define were primarily concerned with, in Nino Frank's phrase, 'the dynamism of violent death',[55] and *Night and the City* of course fits right in. Identifying 'the chase; the hunted man'[56] as the

Fabian's haunted face, the production still that was used on the cover of Borde and Chaumeton's landmark study of film noir

key element in the film that links it to its noir peers, Elia Kazan's *Panic in the Streets* (1950) and John Huston's *The Asphalt Jungle* (1950), they see *Night and the City* as a 'case history'[57] of a traumatised individual, a 'mythomaniac' who will achieve 'psychic liberation' and 'overcome a morbid fear and throw himself into the arms of his executioner'.

Two years later, a feature on Dassin in *Sight & Sound* magazine demonstrated that the UK had begun to catch up with the French interest in him, even if the patronising tone adopted by interviewer Cynthia Grenier couldn't have been more different from Truffaut and Chabrol's awestruck empathy. ('When a big idea comes along ... the thoughts [become] somewhat oversimplified ... In talking to him, it seemed most profitable to stay close to the personal and autobiographical.'[58]) Dassin was already moving away from his noir film: he was then working on his third and final French film (*La Loi*, 1959, with Gina Lollobrigida), shortly before heading off to Greece to make *Never on a Sunday* (1960) with his then girlfriend Melina Mercouri, and so initiating the third period of his remarkable directing career.

Dassin subsequently moved decisively away from the hard-boiled school of film-making that produced *Night and the City*. He made seven films with Mercouri (whom he married in 1966): after *Never on a Sunday*, two drew on classical mythology – *Phaedra* (1962) and *A Dream of Passion* (1978); another was adapted from a then-modish Marguerite Duras novel, *10.30pm Summer* (1966); and one was a bona fide commercial success, the caper movie *Topkapi* (1964). After Mercouri became Minister of Culture in the post-junta Greek government in 1981, neither she nor Dassin made any more films. It was at this point that Dassin visited London for the National Film Theatre event mentioned earlier, where *Rififi* was discussed with enthusiasm, but *Night and the City* entirely ignored.

Jump-cut to the modern day. When Widmark and Dassin died within a few weeks of each other (24 and 31 March 2008, respectively), the coincidence drew superlatives from critics anxious to use *Night and the City* as a touchstone. For example, in Dassin's obituary in *The Independent* newspaper, critic and screenwriter Gilbert Adair called *Night and the City* Dassin's

masterpiece, a bizarrely stylised thriller in which Richard Widmark found himself stalked by Dassin's camera no less than by pursuing mobsters and London, a notoriously un-cinegenic city, was transformed by warped angles and expressionistic lighting into a sinister chequerboard of villainy and terror.[59]

A few days earlier, in Widmark's *Guardian* obituary, critic Ronald Bergan suggested that 'he gave one of his best performances in Jules Dassin's *Night and the City*'.[60] But it wasn't just death-nostalgia: earlier in the decade, the critical chorus of approval had swelled to a roar. In an article for the *Guardian* in 2000, American critic Michael Sragow wrote: 'Dassin's masterpiece … is, I think, the original *Night and the City*, a hard-boiled fable about warped imagination and ambition.'[61] For David Thomson in 2002, the film is 'a brutal noir, much of it shot in real night, and a picture that should have ensured Dassin's future'.[62] Writing in 2001, *Village Voice* critic Elliott Stein called *Night and the City* 'one of the darkest of all noirs and arguably Dassin's best film … Widmark is unforgettable as the crazed, gaunt con man on the run, afraid of every shadow while Dassin's manic *mise en scène* turns all of London into a giant expressionist trap.'[63]

We can ascertain the reawakening of interest in the film in general terms. The 'revisionist noirs' of the late 1960s and early 70s – *Point Blank* (1967), *Klute* (1971), *The Long Goodbye* (1973), *Chinatown* (1974) – were essentially subversive films, where noir tropes were employed to undermine strongly defended social norms. Renewed critical interest in noir emerged simultaneously, with writers like Raymond Durgnat (*Paint It Black*, 1970), Colin McArthur (*Underworld USA*, 1972) and Paul Schrader (*Notes on Film Noir*, 1972), as well as the aforementioned *Film Comment* essay by Place and Peterson in 1974, all of which attempted to define and categorise the style. *Film Noir: An Encyclopaedic Reference* was published in 1979, proof that critics' appetite to try and catalogue noir remained unabated. Film-makers themselves pushed a third wave of interest in noir in the following decade – the so-called 'neo-noir' explosion. *Body Heat* (1981), *Blood Simple* (1984) and *Blue Velvet* (1986) were all films that refashioned noir themes and narratives that deployed motifs and iconography to create exercises in noir style. Later films – *Miller's Crossing* (1990), *Reservoir Dogs* (1992), *LA Confidential* (1997) – triggered a 'retro-noir' wave, films that unashamedly fetishised the original noirs, to the point of mimicry, and studiously focused audiences' attention on their original models. We had our own parallel noir revival in the UK, but on a much smaller scale: *Get Carter* (1971), *The Long Good Friday* (1979) and *Lock Stock and Two Smoking Barrels* (1998) marked the high points of 'revisionist', 'neo' and 'retro' noirs. It was on the back of this last initiative in British cinema that critical works such as Chibnall and Murphy's *British Crime Cinema* (1999) and Andrew Spicer's *Film Noir* (2002), with its extensive chapter on 'British Film Noir', found their niche.

 Night and the City had a peculiar place in all this: its dual status as an Anglo-American noir meant that it was referenced in all treatments of the form. Exactly how will be discussed in the next chapter. But Twentieth Century Fox contributed to the reissue of retro-noir's 'original models' in 1999 by preparing for *Night and the City*'s re-release from the original nitrate. According to Erickson, it was 'rediscovered' in Fox's own vault.[64] Dassin, meanwhile, received considerable attention after the restoration and reissue of *Rififi* (in 1999 in France, 2000 in the US and 2002 in the UK). No one deemed it necessary to stage a full cinematic re-release of *Night and the City*, but it finally emerged as a DVD premiere on the Criterion label in 2005, followed by a British release in 2007 on the BFI label.

2 Night

Film noir

A large part of *Night and the City*'s identity derives, without doubt, from its unique position astride two similar, but far from identical, traditions. It is, as Glenn Erickson puts it, 'a nice piece of connective tissue between American films about the crime underworld and their British counterparts about spivs and other lowlifes'.[65] The most obvious reason *Night and the City* stands tall among other British-made noirs, though, is due to the pedigree of the people involved. Dassin was by far the best known of the key American noir directors to make a film in the UK – though, ironically, his 'namer' Edward Dmytryk had been forced out of Hollywood too, and made the noir-ish *Obsession* (1949) shortly before *Night and the City*. (Dmytryk didn't stick to noir during his time in Britain: he followed *Obsession* with the social-conscience drama *Give Us This Day* aka *Christ in Concrete*, 1949, and the seafaring yarn *Mutiny*, 1952.) It was during the period between these last two films that Dmytryk returned to the US to serve jail time, and then go before HUAC to implicate Dassin. Dmytryk's memoir, *Odd Man Out*, reveals that their animosity did not subside; in his description of a seminar at a 1988 film festival in Barcelona, Dmytryk accuses Dassin of 'insults and lies'[66] in the course of what was clearly an extremely fraught panel discussion about the Hollywood blacklist in which they both took part.

Be that as it may, *Night and the City* is certainly a key film noir; it's in all the guidebooks. But what kind of film noir is it? It bears little resemblance to blood-heat fever dreams like *The Postman Always Rings Twice* and *Laura*, or intricate fables of duplicity such as *The Killers* and *Out of the Past*. In *Film Noir: An Encyclopaedic Reference to the American Style*, Alain Silver zeroes in on the key noir element of doom: '*Night and the City* recruits the formal conventions of film noir to convey an unmistakeable presentiment of fatality.'[67] Fabian, with his jittery ambition and watchful hysteria, is riding for a fall from the very first frame. What have significant critics made of it? In *European Film Noir*, while Andrew Spicer asserts that it's even 'more savage and macabre than its hardboiled American models',[68] Robert Murphy, another contributor to the same book, clearly doesn't rate the film at all: '[Fabian's] schemes never look remotely plausible, and his doom seems less an inevitable descent into tragedy than the casual swatting of a persistent bluebottle'.[69] Kim Newman, writing in the *BFI Companion to Crime*, makes a wider point, asserting that *Night and the City* is 'arguably the best film noir made outside the USA', possessing 'a setting that recalls both Charles Dickens and Dr Mabuse as much as the American noir model'.[70]

These are the orthodox views of *Night and the City*: essentially a localised British variant of a doomed-hustler dissection of quintessential noir provenance. Dassin's participation, especially, reinforces this view, as the man behind *The Naked City* would, it seems, have no trouble in digging into the seamy underbelly of the British capital. *Night and the City* even echoes the title of the earlier, New York-set film, something critics at the time picked up on; the review for *Time and Tide* observed: 'When Jules Dassin arrived in England and expressed confidence in his ability to "do" for London what he "did" for New York in *The Naked City*, it all seemed very promising.'[71] (But, in common with other British critics, *Time and Tide* concluded that he fell short: 'He has failed completely to capture anything like the feel for the place.')

The more closely we examine *Night and the City*, the more we see how attentively Dassin and scriptwriter Eisinger delineated this iconic noir figure. Fabian is an assemblage of hustler tics. His quest for cash is the subject of the first words Mary utters ('You won't find any money there, Harry'). Her second ('Who are you running away from now?') reinforces what we've already seen in the opening scene: Fabian is a man in a hurry. (Actual running had been inextricably linked to hustling in 1941 by Budd Schulberg's Hollywood novel, *What Makes Sammy Run?*) Mary soon tells us about another of the Fabian tics – his permanent state of perspiration: 'You can't go on for ever, always running, always in a sweat.' And finally, his laugh, a modulation of the *Kiss of Death* cackle, erupts at moments of triumph – none more so than at the accompaniment to the 'So you think you've done me in' line, Fabian's final moment of unquenchable hubris. Each scene in *Night and the City* is designed to illuminate one or other of these tics: from Fabian's elaborate wallet-switcheroo con to his smart provocation of the Strangler into agreeing a bout with Nikolas. Fabian's unswerving focus on the hustler life means that, remarkably, he has the least wandering eye of any noir protagonist; to the extent that he is initially baffled as to why Nosseross would want to take revenge on him. (Nosseross, of course, is burning with jealous rage over his wife's attempt to start a relationship with Fabian. Fabian has barely noticed it; as ever, all he's interested in is the money.) In contrast, Fabian's hands-on-drum solo as he enlightens Nosseross about his scheme's success (at the exact point that the Strangler and his manager are signing the contract) is about the most intense erotic experience Fabian has in the entire film.

The carapace of self-interested tics breaks, however, at the moments of stress that propel Fabian to his death. The point at which it all begins to fall apart, where his irreversible slide to death commences, is clearly signposted: the crack of Nikolas's arm as he hits the floor during the wrestlers' three-way brawl. Impelled by some hitherto-undiscovered lack of self-preservation, Fabian launches himself into the ring; for once he is alone, in unavoidable one-on-one combat with someone far more violent than he is prepared or able to be. One forearm smash later, Fabian is history, and can only watch in howling agony as the Strangler and Gregorius fight it out to the death. Fabian's sense of abandonment is amplified to an even greater extent in the much quieter scene that is positioned in the lead-up to the final kill-off: the flash of insight as he sits in Anna O'Leary's

boathouse, exhausted and out of ideas. 'Oh, Anna,' he wails, 'the things I did. The things I did.' Truffaut, for one, found this a scene of great poetry.[72]

Fabian is without doubt marked for death, a dead man walking. The film is splattered with it: the words 'death', 'dead', 'die', 'kill' or 'killed' occur roughly twenty-five times. Serious violence, and the imminent threat of it, is never far away. (The only real debate in *Night and the City* is whether violence should be civilised and rule-bound, like Greco-Roman wrestling, or nasty and brutish, as in catch.) The simmering brutality of course explodes in the still-astonishing five-minute brawl between Gregorius and the Strangler (which is filmed so remorselessly that it seems to go on for half an hour). With its finger jabs, bear hugs and armlocks, the scene still has the capacity to appal at some sixty years distance.

It also throws into sharp relief one of the key issues around *Night and the City*: its commitment to realism. Along with his story about tracking down Zbyszko to a New Jersey chicken farm, Dassin

Anna O'Leary's boathouse on the Thames, where Fabian confronts his failure

explained his attitude to casting him: 'Zanuck wanted me to cast an actor who knew how to wrestle or could appear like a big hulky type. But I wanted a wrestler who could act a bit.'[73] After *The Naked City*, Dassin had acquired a reputation for uncompromising social documentation. Defending the film against the wall-to-wall 'tourist in London' attacks, he pointed out Hoskins's involvement as a location scout: 'I invented nothing; it was all there.'[74] But it's fair to say that his response, if not exactly disingenuous, doesn't really do him, or his film, justice. Even the most casual analysis reveals that Dassin and his DoP Max Greene have harnessed an entire arsenal of expressive visual techniques; in fact, their very profusion means that *Night and the City*'s failures on the authenticity front are considerably masked. It doesn't seem to matter, for example, that Widmark's accent never settles down; far more important is his ability to emote for the camera. (Could any major British actor of the time have managed it? You just can't see James Mason or Richard Attenborough cutting loose in the same way.)

Night and the City, as a consequence, cannot seriously be considered as a sustained attempt at vérité; much more important is its evocation of a symbolic city, the threatening urban maze. As Colin McArthur writes in *Underworld USA*:

The London of *Night and the City* has no temporal or geographical location; it is Thomson's 'city of dreadful night', Warshow's 'dark, sad city of the imagination' ... It is easy to see [Fabian] as the archetypal modern man, running in terror through a dark city.[75]

Foster Hirsch, in *The Dark Side of the Screen: Film Noir*, is even more emphatic:

In its hyperactive transmutations of London into a web of alleys and underground dens, its fevered chiaroscuro, its angular fragmented images, and in Widmark's bravura performance of a born loser ... *Night and the City* may well be the definitive film noir.[76]

Fabian, the man at *Night and the City*'s heart, is the vehicle through which this dread and terror is exposed.

Fabian, however, is not simply a cowering victim of the city. For *Night and the City* is a gangster film, of a sort, and Fabian operates with the drive and momentum common to such films. (The term 'gangster' is used in its loosest sense here; Fabian is pretty much a loner, forming law-breaking alliances and dissolving them as his situation demands.) In his seminal 1948 essay *The Gangster as Tragic Hero*, Robert Warshow outlines the primal conception of the film gangster, which is so close to Dassin and Eisinger's conception of Fabian that it may as well have been used as a script note:

The gangster is the man of the city, with the city's language and knowledge, with its queer and dishonest skills and its terrible daring, carrying his life in his hands like a placard, like a club ... for the gangster there is only the city; he must inhabit it in order to personify it: not the real city, but that dangerous and sad city of the imagination which is so much more important, which is the modern world ... Thrown into the crowd without background or advantages, with only those ambiguous skills which the rest of us ... can only pretend to have, the gangster is required to make his way, to make his life and impose it on others. Usually, when we come upon him, he has already made his choice or the choice has already been made for him.[77]

As this was written only a year before *Night and the City* was filmed, it serves as a guide to the way crime films were understood. Elsewhere in his essay, Warshow makes it clear that he is only thinking of movie gangsters – 'the real city ... produces only criminals; the imaginary city produces the gangster: he is what we want to be and what we are afraid we may become'.[78] Moreover, there is a clear difference between a hustler-weasel like Fabian and the triggermen and punch-up merchants that populate films like *Scarface* (1932) or *The Roaring Twenties* (1939). But it's accurate to say that a hoodlum like Fabian exists as a kind of dream-metaphor; one that has its roots in the quotidian experience of the city, but one freighted with a heightened, intensified paranoia over what may be happening just out of sight or earshot. Fabian's world is familiar – St Martins Lane, Soho, Piccadilly Circus, Hammersmith Bridge – but his experience of it is a counterpoint to what you might call the 'civilian' one. *Night and the City* is like an X-ray – through time as well as space – of the London topography.

In his excellent essay accompanying the Criterion DVD release, Paul Arthur picks up on Warshow's idea, expanding it, even, to suggest that *Night and the City* 'yields the spectre of the "secret city" to which all film noir, regardless of actual setting, pays unspoken tribute'.[79] Noir certainly likes to genericise its depiction of urban environments – flophouses, dive bars, fight halls, walk-up flats – and this has led to extraordinary films like *Sin City* (2005), where design and fantasy have obliterated any trace of the concrete actuality that noir films are rooted in. (With its newspaper-illustration visuals, *Sin City* also appears to have got rid of the actual concrete too.) But *Night and the City*'s London location gives it – like *The Third Man* (1949) and Vienna – a special character, one subtly removed from the dominant American strands. As Charlotte Brunsdon points out in *London in Cinema*, *Night and the City* simultaneously offers 'the generalised urban anomie of film noir'[80] – as exemplified in the 'any night' opening voiceover – and 'a London rendered with some precision'. The overall effect of this is to make *Night and the City* a key example of the 'doubled' setting, where the familiar is made strange as darkness falls. They only come out at night, for sure.

In fact, no one can watch the film without being aware of London's chaotic, run-down state, just five years after the end of World War II. The war is never alluded to in the film – a legacy, no doubt, of the source material, which of course was written before the war began – but evidence of the war and its aftermath is everywhere. The construction sites on the south bank of the Thames (preparing for the Festival of Britain), the corrugated-iron fencing and flattened buildings that Fabian streaks past in sight of St Paul's Cathedral. (However, the only overt allusion to the black market is the bundle of

nylons that Anna O'Leary receives through her boathouse window as she turns down Fabian's plea for money.) If, in the most general sense, we can say that the war reinforced the acceptance of the film noir mood – by admitting previously unthought-of brutalities into ordinary people's lives – then *Night and the City* is one of its most eloquent treatments. It may be considered a weakness that, while the war and its aftermath is a key element in the narrative furniture of *The Third Man*, in *Night and the City* it hovers silently at the fringes. But, like many of the pre-war novels on which classic film noirs were based, the original of *Night and the City* contained a presentiment, a prefiguration of the callousness and brutality to come.

Dassin's own experience of the blacklist certainly ties in with this. His outcast status made him something of a hero to politically inclined film critics, but also gave him an iconic status as a persecuted, isolated artist, and it was something immediately picked up on by the first French analysers of film noir, including Truffaut/Chabrol and

London as an inferno: Fabian runs through a rubble-strewn building site on the South Bank

Borde/Chaumeton. The McCarthy period was a traumatic time for those leftists who saw the war, and America's participation, as a validation; finding themselves the subject of illiberal persecution was – and still is – devastating. The House Un-American Activities Committee had first been established in 1938 as the successor to a series of US congressional bodies designed to investigate internal security. Its initial purpose was to examine pro-Nazi and Ku Klux Klan activists, but even before the war it was summoning suspected communists – like Dassin's boss at the Federal Theater Project, Hallie Flanagan – to testify. The identification of Alger Hiss as a Soviet spy in 1948 gave HUAC's work credibility, but they had already started investigations into the entertainment industry: the Hollywood Ten were, notoriously, named in November 1947. Dassin was not on this particular list, but Edward Dmytryk was, as well as Dalton Trumbo, Ring Lardner Jr and Albert Maltz (writer of *The Naked City*). All ten were convicted of contempt of Congress and served jail time; but Dmytryk was the

A glimpse of modernity: the just-completed Waterloo Bridge is visible in the background as Fabian runs for his life

only one to publicly admit being a communist and give evidence to the Committee in 1951, identifying other members of the party. This was the point at which Dassin was formally named as a communist, but the poisonous atmosphere in Hollywood prior to this had led to the imposition of anti-communist pledges by many organisations, and large numbers of dismissals; hence Zanuck's concern to get Dassin out of the US in mid-1949.

The spectre of the blacklist looms large over *Night and the City*, and its influence on readings of the film is inescapable. Given how bound up Dassin's flight from HUAC was with its inception, it's hardly a surprise. Paul Arthur suggests that 'Fabian's predicament [is] in part Dassin's allegorical response to his own hasty emigration',[81] while in Glenn Erickson's opinion, 'the film itself appears to be a fugitive from McCarthyism'.[82] While these assertions are clearly not the case in the literal sense, there's no doubt that, in hindsight, *Night and the City*'s hysteria-driven energy, largely deriving from Widmark's performance, parallels the position Dassin and many others found themselves in. Nicholas Christopher, in *Somewhere in the Night*, goes even further and contends that the film's 'London is a shadow-city, a stand-in for the American city he has left behind'.[83] If so, this would accord with the generalised, fabular view of the noir narrative; what happens in *Night and the City* could have happened anywhere. This is only partly true.

Visual style

One of the main methods of reinforcing noir themes, and establishing *Night and the City*'s connection with the international body of noir cinema, is in the application of the chiaroscuro, expressionism-influenced visual style designed to evoke the traumatised mind-sets of the typical noir protagonist. *Night and the City* is no exception. But equally, *Night and the City* isn't only about high-contrast lighting and skewed angles; Dassin skilfully deploys vérité (the drive around Piccadilly Circus, for example) and nakedly religious symbolism to heighten the drama.

CORNERS: The characteristic Fabian pose: at bay, in close-up, checking over his shoulder or peering around corners

ANGLES: Fabian sprints past the front steps of St Paul's Cathedral, a high-angled shot of a man in trouble; here is humanity as an insect, ripe for obliteration

Another high angle, denoting pursuit and paranoia. Note how tightly framed the waiting figure is; it makes him more threatening

SPACE: Another of Fabian's characteristic depictions: he's nothing more than a rat up a drainpipe. A frontal shot of an alleyway, barely wide enough to take a human being. Backlighting at the far end emphasises length and narrowness

Stairwells can express entrapment too: just stick the camera at the top and shoot downwards. Backlighting is a vital part of the effect

Fabian runs for his life. Tilted camera, jarring shapes, shadows everywhere; the suggestion of a gibbet above. Expressionist menace par excellence

SHADOWS: The shadow of Fabian's pursuer looms outside his refuge like Nosferatu creeping up the stairs: a primitive but effective image derived from classic Expressionist cinema

The shadow cast by a hat, lit from above, is a useful way to indicate moral turpitude. Fabian is about to try and filch money from his girlfriend's purse

Fabian at bay under the railway arches. Shadows on the wall increase the threat levels

OFF FRAME: A smart composition: the cabbie leans into frame to tip Fabian off about his clueless fares, making clear the surreptitious nature of the exchange

The Strangler launches his attack from off screen, grabbing Fabian by the throat in close-up and stopping him short. A brutal, jolting end

VÉRITÉ: Yosh spreads the word in Piccadilly Circus. Fixed-camera vérité; a highly perspectivised shot borrowed from *Gun Crazy*

MENACE: Extreme close-up immediately establishes Kristo's threat; Gregorius doesn't come across as a pushover either

A subtle bit of visual presentiment: Gregorius in front of the image of the man who will kill him

VIOLENCE: The
Strangler vs. Gregorius;
brutality rendered in
monumental close-up,
every finger dig, head
lock, bear hug seen in
eye-watering detail

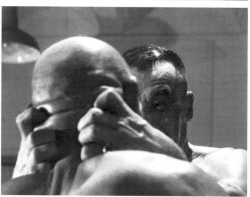

BEAST: The extraordinary image of Nosseross smelling the fur he's given to his wife. The shadows on the ceiling tell us this is a cage, a trap, a beast in its lair

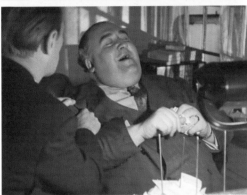

A grotesque Nosseross cackling deliriously. Lit from below, emphasising his bulk; and the vertical spikes tell us once again that this is a trap for the unwary

A carefully placed light on the floor of a bus – and Nosseross's evil comes out yet again, as he prepares to stitch Fabian up

DERANGEMENT: Fabian retreating from a confidently vindictive Nosseross. The lighting tells you everything about Fabian's perturbed state

Fabian waits for the end. The light picks out his eyes; he is seeing clearly now

SACRIFICE: Christian imagery seeps in: here is Fabian as Christ, broken after deposition from the Cross

Here Fabian is arranged after Christ's entombment – the Strangler is about to throw Fabian into the river

Kristo as Pilate, dispensing justice. He looms high in the frame, redolent with power; the neo-classical architecture of the bridge is an unconscious reinforcement of the Imperial symbolism

3 The City

Soho

Greek and Frith, Dean and D'Arblay; Wardour, Poland, Carnaby and Rupert; Berwick, Broadwick, Beak and Brewer; Old Compton, Great Windmill and Great Marlborough ... these are the Soho streets: a roll-call of the damned. Their pavements are worn by centuries of pounding, their stairwells packed with thousands of walk-up flats, their streetlamps dimly sputtering in the urban murk. Soho is an onion: the more you peel it, the more layers you find. Or, put another way, it is a palimpsest in its classic definition: a manuscript scraped clean and reused. Over the centuries, Soho has been the site of aristocratic sleaze, immigrant struggle, gang warfare, peep-show smut, bohemian camaraderie, cinema-world gruesome killings, the pink pound – all overlaid, one on top of the other. A few short streets contained The Fight That Never Was, Freddie Mills, the Cave of the Golden Calf, Harry Roy's Bat Club Boys, Mr Young's, the 86, Ham Yard, Tony Tenser. The names are legion. Soho is the map, canvas and stage-set for *Night and the City*, the interzone of the imagination where high tragedy is reinvented as a wide-boy razor ballet. Kersh's Fabian hardly sets foot outside the Soho square mile, except for a schvitz in a steam bath on York Way, before cabbing up to the suburbs to chisel a hapless office drone.

In previous sections of this book, the emphasis has been on what *Night and the City* has in common with the current of international film noir. But it's also a product of a distinctively British cultural tradition, one that relies heavily on its setting, the central London district of Soho. By the time Dassin was finished, Soho was still there in the background of the movie; even if Dassin went south, west and east for the most picturesque scenes. Fabian takes on a knifeman in Lambeth, runs for his life in Ludgate, has his neck

broken in Hammersmith, fakes Helen's club licence in County Hall in Waterloo; but Dassin knew enough to settle him in the West End for his finagling and flim-flamming. The 'Fabian Promotions' sign is raised in Great Windmill Street – the doorway beneath it has vanished, replaced by a remodelled shopfront for a café selling Thai food. The legendary Café Anglais in Leicester Square doubled as the American Bar, where Fabian puts the moves on the trio of rubes. He heads across St Martins Lane to Goodwins Court to try his luck with Nosseross, downstairs in the Silver Fox. (Technically, it's in Covent Garden, but only by a few yards.) And he holes up with Mary in her one-room place in crummy Richmond Buildings. (Never one to miss a trick, Dassin cheats his way through the scene the first time Harry sprints into view; astute camera placement means Richmond Buildings doesn't look like a cul-de-sac. We get the reverse angle much later, when Adam grabs a taxi outside, and see the glowering bulk of car dealer Shaw & Kilburn's building at the end of the street. Now it's a hotel.)

The view down Great Windmill Street in Soho as Fabian's beloved sign is lowered into position

Dassin liked his vérité shots, and there's an unexpected bonus: whenever he had to take his crew out onto the West End streets, closing them off completely was impossible. So the film contains banks of goggle-eyed passers-by, stopping to watch the Hollywooders go about their business. Mostly they line up as if watching a cricket game – see how they jam the kerb in front of the Café de l'Europe as Harry's marks arrive in Leicester Square in a taxi (a taxi! try that today) – but sometimes you get honest-to-goodness astonishment, like the well-bred gent waiting to cross Piccadilly Circus who gives us an icy glare as Yosh stops to bend the ear of the paper-seller. Dassin may have had to rely on Percy Hoskins to show him around, but his film possesses those corner-of-the-eye glimpses that are gold. However, he presumably didn't need much help for the opening-credit clipshow of gloomy tourist locations: the Thames Embankment, Tower Bridge, Trafalgar Square, the Houses of Parliament, which are explicitly contrasted with the more orthodox

Fabian waits on Westminster Bridge, just by County Hall, as Helen arrives by taxi

noir vision of the city as an elemental shadowy menace. In *London in Cinema*, Brunsdon identifies this as the essence of the 'double-faced West End':

There are two Londons in this film: and the way they are mapped over each other makes it impossible, by the end of the film, to see the first London, a public, tourist, landmark West End London, without understanding the way in which it is subtended by another London, one of graft, pay-offs and the hierarchy of the underworld.[84]

In an informative, if occasionally impenetrable, book called *Nights in the Big City*, German academic Joachim Schlör elaborates on exactly this subject: how the creation of the modern city changed and deepened its inhabitants' relationship with the night. Taking Paris, Berlin and London as his principal examples, Schlör identifies the 1840s as the period during which the modern city came into existence. London, he suggests, was the first (at least of the three major European capitals), the mass migrations of the Industrial Revolution being primarily responsible. The huge numbers of people that came into cities were responsible for the creation of 'night life' – a broader concept than simply nightclub-based entertainment. Early morning produce marketeers, night-time street cleaners, 24-hour policing: all contributed to the extension of the active life of the city, which had remained essentially unchanged since the medieval practice of shutting down at sundown. But the development of artificial light – gas, naptha, electricity – only reinforced the special nature of the life of the night. (London's first gas street lighting was set up in Pall Mall in 1807; electrics arrived in Holborn in the 1870s.) James Thomson's celebrated 1874 poem *The City of Dreadful Night* is not shy of exploiting the gloomy desolation that night-lighting can bring.

The street-lamps always burn; but scarce a casement
In house or palace front from roof to basement
Doth glow or gleam athwart the mirk air cast.

The street-lamps burn amid the baleful glooms,
Amidst the soundless solitudes immense
Of ranged mansions dark and still as tombs.[85]

By the time Kersh was writing, though, the nocturnal city – and Soho specifically – had been given its own aesthetic identity by the flâneurs and night-walkers of the nineteenth century. Charles Dickens was probably the most famous: his urban ramblings were collected in 1861 in *The Uncommercial Traveller*: 'Walking the streets under the pattering rain, [I] would walk and walk and walk, seeing nothing but the interminable tangle of streets, save at a corner, here and there, two policemen in conversation, or the sergeant or inspector looking after his men.'[86] Venturing near Soho, he has one of his most spectral encounters:

I came to the great steps of St Martin's church as the clock was striking Three. Suddenly, a thing that in a moment more I should have trodden upon without seeing, rose up at my feet with a cry of loneliness … It shivered from head to foot, and its teeth chattered, and as it stared at me – persecutor, devil, ghost, whatever it thought me – it made with its whining mouth as if it were snapping at me, like a worried dog.[87]

Dickens, though, was not the originator of the theme of Soho as the nineteenth-century harbour of destitution; forty years earlier, Thomas de Quincey's *Confessions of an English Opium Eater* recalled his time as a homeless runaway in 1802 or 1803. De Quincey experienced Soho as a bewilderingly erratic environment, where desperation and normality exist side by side. He finds in Soho 'darkness, cold, silence, and desolation'; he befriends a fifteen-year-old streetwalker called Ann, who saves his life one night when he collapses in Soho Square. But de Quincey is always conscious of the evolving urban environment: he recalls 'gazing from Oxford Street up every avenue in succession which pierces through the heart of Marylebone to the fields and the woods'; he returns, a few years later, to the derelict house in which he nearly starved to death, finding it 'now occupied by a respectable family'; and when Ann accompanies him to the mail coach to escape London's toxic atmosphere, he remembers:

Our course lay through a part of the town which has now all disappeared, so that I can no longer retrace its ancient boundaries – Swallow Street, I think it was called. Having time enough before us, however, we bore away to the left until we came into Golden Square; there, near the corner of Sherrard Street, we sat down, not wishing to part in the tumult and blaze of Piccadilly.[88]

Here we can see the unmistakable community of the night's inhabitants, as well as the particular geography of their wanderings through a city whose physical evolution was unstoppable. And if a physical location can be haunted by emotional trauma, then it's probably best to steer clear of the junction of Oxford Street and Great Titchfield Street; it's here that de Quincey made a loose arrangement to meet Ann if he returned to London – but he never saw her again, despite his habitual visits to their meeting place.

Other writers contributed to Soho flâneur-ism: after World War II, travel writer Stephen Graham took it upon himself to examine London as if it was as strange as Crimean Russia (Berwick Street market was 'a wild and desolate scene, like the bed of the rotten sea'[89]) and during World War II, Thomas 'Limehouse Nights' Burke produced a semi-nostalgic description of London entertainments past that the privations of the Blitz were currently denying the West End (Soho drinking clubs were mostly 'a swarm of shabby little two-room places, in West End cellars', making 'the term night club disreputable again'.[90] No change there, then.)

But Kersh picked up on de Quincey's idea that the convergence of streets that was Piccadilly was London's heart: he wrote that Fabian 'saw London as a kind of Inferno – a series of concentric areas with Piccadilly Circus as the ultimate centre'. But *Night and the City* lay at the other side of modernism from *Confessions of an Opium*

Eater, and Kersh chronicled the eroticised life of the streets with Dickensian attack:

In Regent Street and Shaftesbury Avenue the traffic-streams grew thicker, and slowed down ... There was an atmosphere of panic: you thought of Sodom under the thunderbolts. In Rupert Street, jammed bumper to bumper, a line of quivering cars waited for the lights to change. Under the shaky scarlet light of the neon signs, Chrysler nuzzled Austin and Morris sniffed at the hindquarters of Ford, as if that humid spring night had brought about some nightmarish mating-season of machines – some madman's vision of the coupling of panting iron beasts in a burning jungle of stone.[91]

This modernist vision of the city as organism was too good a cue to miss for Dassin, who made much of the illuminations in Piccadilly Circus – Wrigley's, Bovril, Schweppes, Guinness Is Good for You – as emblems of London's buzzing modernity. In this, he was simply

'A blazing veinwork of neon-tubes': Piccadilly Circus as seen in *Night and the City*'s title sequence

reflecting Kersh: Piccadilly Circus had been known for its electric signs since 1910, and in his novel, Kersh writes: 'West Central started to flare and squirm in a blazing veinwork of neon-tubes. Bursting like inexhaustible fireworks, the million coloured bulbs of the electric signs blazed in perpetual recurrence over the face of the West End.'[92] The neon glow of Piccadilly's signs are the chief metonym of the artificial day, the electric yellow glow that cocoons the Londoner against the lightless blanket of night. It's only if you look carefully at *Night and the City* that can you see something of London's genuine modernity: a couple of brief glimpses of the recently completed Waterloo Bridge as Fabian dashes away from the Shot Tower. The gleaming concrete spans are a sudden irruption of the future in a cinematic vision that favours the battered and decrepit.

Lowlife fiction

This dramatic urban landscape is the backdrop to, and originator of, a brand of British writing that forms the bedrock of *Night and the City* both as novel and film. Lowlife fiction – a term popularised by modern fans of the genre – is the crucible in which *Night and the City* was forged. Many of them became films: James Curtis's *There Ain't No Justice*, Robert Westerby's *Wide Boys Never Work*, Graham Greene's *Brighton Rock*. Whether as melancholic fable, working-class consciousness or pulp thriller, the lowlife novel is one of the major overlooked strands of twentieth-century fiction. And it's very Soho.

Patrick Hamilton was one of the first writers to apply literary style to Soho flâneurie: *The Midnight Bell*, published in 1929, distils the tenor of Hamilton's own life in the 1920s. A precisely calibrated story of failure, frustration and bitterness, it set a precedent for the exploitation of lowlife tropes – streetwalkers, drinkers, pavement-pounding, electric light – that others would follow. Soho, first and foremost, stands as a zone of sexual licence and freedom; it's here that timid, intellectual bartender Bob can gawp at the women selling themselves, and even fall in love – with Jenny, who 'really didn't look like one'. Here's the passage where Bob wanders the Soho streets:

It was still a little too early to go and eat, and anyway the streets were far too fascinating to leave. He again entered Wardour Street, and walked up towards Shaftesbury Avenue. Bob was always diverted by Wardour Street, because it was the principal resort of the women of the town. To him, as with most young men, of whatever class, the poisonous horror of their bearing yet bore the glamour and beauty of the macabre, even if he prided himself that he was superior to adventure of this kind.[93]

The Midnight Bell never became a feature film; British cinema, perhaps, wasn't quite ready for it. James Curtis, however, was more successful at staking out the territory Kersh's novel was to follow. Curtis, a dyed-in-the-wool socialist who was a product of public school, weighed in with a pre-war trilogy of now-celebrated crime novels: *The Gilt Kid* (1936), about a housebreaker; *There Ain't No Justice* (1937), about a young boxer; and *They Drive by Night* (1938), about an ex-convict on the run. The last two were turned into films before the war and became standard-bearers of a new mood of British hard-boiled realism. In *They Drive by Night* (1938) (not to be confused with the Bogart film of the same title), Emlyn Williams (the playwright!) struggles to clear his name of a murder actually committed by creepy sophisticate Ernest Thesiger. *There Ain't No Justice* was the directorial debut of British cinema's golden boy Pen Tennyson, and starred a fresh-faced Jimmy Hanley trying to stay straight in the boxing game. Neither approaches the narrative sophistication of *Night and the City* – both films are still very much straitjacketed by the conventions of moral melodrama – but it was a start.

The gap between cinema and novel is still very evident. For the authentic street flavour of the 1930s, you still have to go back to the printed page. *The Gilt Kid* spends three chapters detailing a pub crawl:

The evening bustle was well under way. He would, he decided, go up into Shaftesbury Avenue and have a drink or so in one of the wallopers there. It was more than likely that he would bump into one of the boys … he walked slowly down towards Lisle Street. He was feeling good and lit up.[94]

Curtis also introduces copious amounts of street slang, which was to become a staple of British crime novels and films in later decades. *The Gilt Kid* is full of it: 'jane', 'kite', 'steamer', 'screw', 'oncer', 'tightener', 'ronce', 'ribs', 'slop'. Curtis even gets the phrase 'wide boy' in, well before Westerby's *Wide Boys Never Work* (1937) allegedly invented the term.

Even if they don't always agree on exact terms and definitions, Kersh follows Curtis in luxuriating in this idiosyncratic London street code. It's one of the film adaptation's great losses: made for an international audience, and by an American team who presumably were not willing or able to get to grips with it, the film completely loses Kersh's version of the underworld argot. In the novel of *Night and the City*, Fabian is a linguistically confusing figure, mixing American slang – 'swell', 'red-hot', 'cinch' – with local argot; it's the key to his divided character. All of this has been eradicated from Dassin's film; but neither does it show up in British film treatments of the era. *Wide Boys Never Work* was a celebrated literary product of its day, but it took until 1956 for a film version to emerge: *Soho Incident*, or *Spin a Dark Web*, as it was known in the US. Like *Night and the City*, *Soho Incident* hit on the questionable idea of bringing in an overseas face, Canadian actor Lee Patterson, to Americanise the lead role of an aspiring hustler who makes his way through the London lowlife. In *Street of Shadows* (1953), Laurence Meynell's wartime pulp potboiler *The Creaking Chair* is almost entirely transformed into a psycho-noir, with rudimentary attempts to evoke the disturbed state of mind of its killer. As source material, *The Creaking Chair* was, however, pretty thin stuff compared to Kersh's *Night and the City*: a fictionalised Soho with an impossibly gentlemanly pin-table parlour owner (called Lou Steel, more like Richard Hannay than Harry Fabian) who fascinates, and is fascinated by, aristocratic Barbara Gale.

Arguably, the most influential writer of lowlife novels is, of course, Graham Greene, whose *A Gun for Sale* and *Brighton Rock* elevated the literary status of the genre. Although *A Gun for Sale*

(1936) is essentially a political fable, hitman Raven holes up in a small room off Frith Street. Attainable sex is the dominant Soho motif, and Raven's disgust is played out on the same streets as Kersh, Curtis and Hamilton's. *Brighton Rock* was published in the same year as *Night and the City* and is not, clearly, set in Soho, but nevertheless partakes in all the well-established lowlife rituals: a squealer is killed, and the hoodlum must dispose of the evidence. (And, like Raven, Pinkie's callousness is presented as a consequence of his sexual terror.) Both novels became films: *A Gun for Sale* went across the Atlantic to become *This Gun for Hire* (1942), an Alan Ladd hitman movie that is about as far from its source material as *Night and the City*. *Brighton Rock*, on the other hand, was directed by the Boulting brothers and gave Richard Attenborough his first major starring role. As Greene collaborated on the screenplay with Terence Rattigan, he could ensure that much of his novel survived intact. The film manages to combine some authentically smelly gangster material with a consideration of the spiritual traumas that preoccupy Pinkie in the novel. Here we have *Night and the City* in embryonic form: the hoodlum as existential hero, heading unthinkingly towards his own destruction.

Spivs

Brighton Rock is also a reminder of what has come to be called 'the spiv cycle', a group of British films tapping into the social exhaustion and destabilised class system that characterised post-war Britain. *Night and the City* fits squarely in this cycle, but 'spiv' is one word you won't hear in the film, the one that gave it its identity, topicality and charge. The spiv, of course, is well known to generations of Brits, a wartime black-marketeer, a ducker and diver in a flash suit and fedora hat, a ferrety deal-maker who nevertheless avoided punch-ups wherever possible. The spiv was identified as a social type well before the war: John Worby's 1937 *Autobiography of a Spiv* defines him as 'a man who gets a good living by his wits without working'.[95] While soon to become a comic character – George Cole in the St Trinian's films;

James Beck in *Dad's Army* – before that, the spiv, aka 'wide boy', was a potent, if hardly fear-inspiring, figure in the British underworld.

In *British Crime Cinema*, Chibnall and Murphy make the point that, in the early days, British film-makers were 'chary of showing too much sympathy for the criminal ... the spiv cycle of the late 40s can be seen as the first surge of an indigenous British underworld genre'.[96] Peter Wollen, in particular, has written at length about the spiv movie in *Paris Hollywood*. 'Spiv itself seems to have been as much a fashion term as a job description',[97] while the spiv cycle, he suggested, allowed film-makers 'to explore the darker, more sinister side of Britishness without losing touch with the lived experience of the street and the community'. But spiv films don't automatically engage with the darkly subversive themes of film noir. The first spiv film that Wollen identifies, in his essay 'Riff Raff Realism', is the 1944 Cary Grant vehicle, *None but the Lonely Heart*. Its provenance is remarkably similar to *Night and the City*: a popular British novel picked up by a Hollywood studio (in this case, RKO) and given to an American director and star to complete. (The director, it should be pointed out was Clifford 'Waiting for Lefty' Odets, the radical playwright who so entranced Dassin in the early days; but like Eisinger, Odets's talents didn't translate.) In Richard Llewellyn's original novel, published in 1943, central character Ernie Mott is a disillusioned young printworker who abandons his dreams of being a painter after stumbling into petty crime. (Kersh operates a similar obverse/reverse correlation between art and crime in *Night and the City*, through the character of Adam.) Odets and Grant convert the story into a cockney picaresque, with Mott now a one-time drifter settling back down in the East End. Grant, reputedly, saw *None but the Lonely Heart* as his best performance, streets ahead of his default light-comedy mode. But in Dick Van Dyke cap and neckerchief, his version of Mott is nothing like the brash figure that Llewellyn described.

In his essay about *The Third Man*, delineating the slippage between spivs and spies, Wollen sums up the attraction of spivs – both to society at large, and film-makers in particular:

In essence, [they] represented a mutation in the traditional British crime film that took place in response to the changing pattern of crime itself, where state regulation of the economy, rationing and rising prices had led inevitably to the emergence of a black market ... The crucial difference between the spiv – a flashy black-marketeer – and the classic gangster was the degree of sympathy the spiv attracted among audiences weary of wartime and post-war shortages: black-marketeers may have been outside the law, but they performed an obvious public service. They could even become heroes.[98]

The spiv, Wollen tells us, exists 'in a world marked by illegality, subterfuge and betrayal, being at all times a man on the run'. Though he is writing about Harry Lime, it couldn't be a more apt description of Harry Fabian. In *Realism and Tinsel*, Robert Murphy is even more direct about the relationship between the two films:

The success of *The Third Man* encouraged Twentieth Century Fox to try their hand at an up-market spiv movie ... [*Night and the City*] fared badly at the box office and, as hostile criticism had not harmed the prospects of earlier spiv films, this indicates public tastes were changing, an impression reinforced by the huge success of *The Blue Lamp*.[99]

Brighton Rock is also clearly identifiable as a spiv film, as is *They Made Me a Fugitive*, another noirish story that used the experience of the war to toughen up its moral universe. Trevor Howard plays an airman adrift since returning from fighting who becomes entangled with a vicious gangster through sheer boredom. Unlike *Night and the City*, however, *They Made Me a Fugitive* specifically cites the effect of the war as the source of Howard's moral dislocation; in Dassin's film, it's a never-mentioned background factor that we have to infer. *Noose* (1948), taken from another Richard Llewellyn original (a hit stage play), is a much more orthodox thriller than *None but the Lonely Heart* (which feels like *This Sporting Life* or *Saturday Night and Sunday Morning* by comparison). *Noose* features Carole Landis, in one of her last screen appearances, as a sparky reporter attempting to pin a murder on greasy Italian spiv Sugiani, whose downfall is sealed by a team of tough but honest British sportsmen. (Wartime emotions were still obviously running high.) By contrast, in the above-mentioned *Street of Shadows*, the foreign spiv, played by Cesar Romero, had actually mutated into the good guy.

The spiv cycle began to falter in the mid-1950s. Chibnall and Murphy again:

> By the early 1950s, the trends that had shaped the spiv movies had run their course. From the late 1940s to the mid-1950s, the crime rate fell, the police force was built up to its pre-war strength and the underworld settled down, as deserters were integrated back into society.[100]

Even so, the spiv movie didn't go away until the early 1960s: Ken Hughes's *The Small World of Sammy Lee* (1963) arrived as the wide-boy culture was already on its last legs, displaced by the 1960s' enfranchisement of the working classes to the fashionable demi-monde. Even if it is a throwback, its story of Anthony Newley's Soho fast-talker trying to raise money in a hurry achieves a lightness and momentum that earlier films never managed. But after that, the spiv was history.

Where does *Night and the City* fit? Fabian is never identified as a spiv: partly because Kersh's novel was written before the term achieved wide currency, and partly because the subtleties of the term were clearly lost on the film's American writer and director. In his hounds-tooth suit and snap-brim hat, Fabian demonstrates plenty of spiv characteristics – such as his exhibitionist tipping – but in truth, it's all generic-hustler stuff. Unable to grapple with the rudiments of street chat that littered Kersh's novel (and which was de rigueur for all comparable British pulps), *Night and the City*'s relationship with actual spivdom is somewhat at a distance.

Crime

Another factor plays its part in how we respond to *Night and the City*: its connection with what you might call 'reality'. Audiences saw in *The Blue Lamp* an authentic depiction of contemporary London; reviewers, as we have already seen, sneered at what they saw as an implausible London underworld. Were they right? Petty crime being what it is, it's hard to take any memoir at face value; self-serving to a fault, hoodlums, gangsters and wide boys are the archetype of unreliable narrators. James Morton, the former solicitor turned crime-world chronicler, has focused on Soho in one of his *Gangland* series, and the picture he draws is of an area overrun by 'the chaps': founded on the vice and protection trade, infiltrated by drug dealers, and the point at which many dubious enterprises overlapped. In the pre-war period when *Night and the City* was written, the Sabini racetrack gang ran Soho's protection, while 'white birding' – the fate Fabian plans for his girl Zoe – was rife from the 1920s onwards. (Morton describes a French pimp named Juan Antonio Castanar, who sold girls to overseas 'dance troupes' for £50 each. He also arranged for foreign prostitutes to marry English-born tramps and the like, to ensure they could gain citizenship.) In fact, the period just prior to *Night and the City*'s publication saw a string of vicious prostitute murders in Soho, and the arrival of the Maltese family, the Messinas, who quickly took control of the area's vice.

But World War II signalled big changes in Soho. The Sabini family, émigrés from Italy, were quickly interned as enemy aliens, leaving a patchwork of hoodlums to fight it out on the streets. Figures like Albert Dimes, Jack Spot and Billy Hill were the new names. (The murder of Little Hubby Distelman in 1941 in a billiard club on Wardour Street demonstrated the increasing level of inter-gang violence.) Hill, in particular, profited from the black market, and then began organising armed robberies on an ever-increasing scale. (His first really successful job was the notorious Eastcastle Street mailbag robbery in 1952, in north Soho, which netted over £250,000. It was quickly fictionalised in a cod-noir James Hadley Chase novel, *The Things Men Do*.) Of equal urgency, in the immediate post-war period, was the surge in juvenile delinquency and outbursts of sometimes deadly violence. One case in particular –

the killing of passer-by Alec de Antiquis during a robbery in 1947 –
became the lightning rod of social paranoia. Soho was, as usual,
the centre of attention: the murder took place in Charlotte Street,
as de Antiquis tried to stop three villains (aged between seventeen
and twenty-three) fleeing after holding up a pawnshop in Tottenham
Street. Guns were freely available after the war, as servicemen
brought them home from the fighting (the principal market in
firearms was via the dodgy dealers in Ham Yard, off Great Windmill
Street).

On the evidence, then, Widmark's crafty hustling is hardly
authentic; no wonder reviewers preferred *The Blue Lamp*, which
tapped more obviously into urgent social malaise. Moreover, as is
readily apparent, post-war Soho was increasingly being annexed by
bohemian society, and memoirs by the likes of Daniel Farson (*Soho in
the Fifties*) describe a world very different from *Night and the City*.
Then again, this may not have been entirely the case: Frank Norman's
1959 memoir *Stand on Me* evokes a Soho far more Kersh-esque than
might have been supposed to have survived. Norman went on to
write *Fings Ain't Wot They Used T'be* two years later, using the same
material; hoodlums, razor-boys, bent coppers, etc. But Norman's
Soho is *Night and the City* reborn: Norman even has a spell – and it
must be the early 1950s – as a Fabian-style club tout:

I mean, a clip joint in a back street, in fact nothing but a hole in the ground
where they sold near beer and had a few flash looking birds who geed up the
customers into spending all their money ... I got paid strictly on commission,
if I got mugs into the gaff I got paid, if I didn't I got nisht a penny.[101]

And while Norman didn't attempt to break into wrestling, his time as
a tout saw him ending up getting cut badly by a rival gang.

Conclusion

All the above – the international noir style, the mythologising of
Soho, lowlife fiction, the 'spiv cycle' and true crime – feed into

Night and the City's status as one of the great British film noirs. Made by Americans, shot in England, *Night and the City*'s peculiar position is that it straddled many worlds; in his section of *British Crime Cinema*, Tim Pulleine concludes that 'a transatlantic ambience envelops the film'.[102] This is certainly the case, on even a cursory examination, but British noir is part of its own mini-tradition, one that, like *Night and the City* itself, is caught between the desire to emulate the supra-national, emotion-focused Hollywood manner, and the instinct to fasten on to home-grown specifics and places.

One of *Night and the City*'s most interesting forerunners in this regard is the film generally accepted as the first British noir:[103] *The Green Cockatoo*, filmed in 1937 from a Graham Greene script and starring John Mills. Mutz Greenbaum, later to become *Night and the City*'s Max Greene, was the cinematographer. Such a key document of British cinema history really deserves looking out: it's an entertaining, if hardly complex, crime story planted in a set-bound Soho, the location of the eponymous nightclub. Mills plays Jim Connor, the sharp-suited owner of the club, whose brother Dave (Robert Newton) has done the dirty on some racetrack villains and is stabbed for his trouble. Winsome René Ray, a country gal adrift in the big city, must avoid the murderous gang and get word to Jim, as well as avoid the police, who think she killed Newton. (It wasn't released until 1940: the three-year delay was down to the distributors' reluctance 'to expose the audience to anything resembling the reality of the criminal underworld'.[104]) *The Green Cockatoo* may have sold itself on its verisimilitude but, at this distance, the film remains very firmly in the uncomplicated world of the good-guy/bad-guy thriller. Its Soho milieu is the main point of connection with *Night and the City*; nowhere does it try to develop the brooding atmosphere or doomed fatalism of the later film.

Night and the City also draws on British noir's habit of invoking a connection with Gothic and late-Victorian literary tradition. It's an idiosyncrasy that underpins David Lean's adaptations of *Great*

Expectations (1946) and *Oliver Twist*, Robert Hamer's pub-set *Pink String and Sealing Wax* and the Patrick Hamilton adaptation *Gaslight* (1940), directed by Thorold Dickinson. There are traces of this in *Night and the City* in its own Dickensian elements: most notably in Figler's Fagin-esque army of beggars, as well as an array of smaller characters – Chilk the lawyer, Googin the forger ('I'm just helpless. Just plain, sprawlin' helpless') and Beer the fight coach. (Yosh, Chilk's minder, is equally Dickensian, and is one of the few survivals from Kersh's original novel.)

Moreover, *Night and the City* emulates topographically dense British noirs like *It Always Rains on Sunday*, which, like Odets/Grant *None but the Lonely Heart*, is intended at least partly to be a portrait of a specific community, with multiple storylines criss-crossing the same stretch of tarmac. *It Always Rains on Sunday* contains Googie Withers's third great noir role: she plays a Bethnal Green housewife who rashly decides to hide her escaped-convict former lover in the

Dawn breaks over Hammersmith as Fabian spots his nemesis on the bridge

attic. It's a much more downbeat film than *Night and the City*, playing to the strengths of unflashy character drama, but it adds a certain poetic, lyrical quality to the realism it aspires to. It certainly beats *None but the Lonely Heart* hands down in terms of its commitment to authenticity. *Night and the City* is a film with things to say about London in general, but also about the square mile of Soho in particular.

But *Night and the City*'s real comparison, and partner in crime, is *The Third Man*, in which Graham Greene's brilliantly imagined bait-and-switch device (of the unexplained figure in the dark) then folds back to reveal a narrative as demonic as *Heart of Darkness*. Both films share a cinematic texture in which the fabric of the city that surrounds them infects every second of their existence, and warps and deforms the ambitions of the people who inhabit them. *Night and the City* does all this without leaving London; nothing else has ever come close.

Notes

1 James Morton, *Gangland: London's Underworld* (London: Warner, 1992), p. 34.

2 Ibid., p. 3.

3 John King, 'Foreword', in Gerald Kersh, *Night and the City* (London: London Books, 2007), p. 10.

4 On-stage NFT interview, 14 July 2002.

5 Tim Pulleine, 'Spin a Dark Web', in Steve Chibnall and Robert Murphy (eds), *British Crime Cinema* (London: Routledge, 1999), p. 33.

6 Paul Duncan, Audio commentary, *Night and the City* DVD (BFI, 2007).

7 Margaret Dickinson and Sarah Street (eds), *Cinema and State: The Film Industry and the British Government 1927–1984* (London: BFI, 1985), p. 190.

8 *New York Times*, 1 April 2008.

9 Filmed interview, *Night and the City* DVD.

10 Sandra Berg, 'When Noir Turned Black', *Written By* magazine, November 2006.

11 Patrick McGilligan (ed.), *Tender Comrades: A Backstory of the Hollywood Blacklist* (New York: St Martin's Press, 1997), p. 208.

12 Berg, 'When Noir Turned Black'.

13 McGilligan, *Tender Comrades*, p. 206.

14 Berg, 'When Noir Turned Black'.

15 McGilligan, *Tender Comrades*, p. 208.

16 Filmed interview, *Night and the City* DVD.

17 Ibid.

18 Foster Hirsch, *The Dark Side of the Screen* (Cambridge, MA: Da Capo Press, 2001), p. 160.

19 Filmed interview, *Night and the City* DVD.

20 John McCallum, *Life with Googie* (London: Heinemann, 1979), p. 7.

21 *The Independent*, 18 December 2004.

22 Filmed interview, *Night and the City* DVD.

23 Ibid.

24 Ibid.

25 Ibid.

26 Ibid.

27 Ibid.

28 Christopher Husted, Booklet essay, *Night and the City: The Two Scores* CD (SAE-CRS-00088, 2003).

29 Ibid.

30 <www.dvdtalk.com/dvdsavant/s1493city.html>.

31 Glenn Erickson, 'Expressionist Doom in Night and the City', in Alain Silver and James Ursini (eds), *Film Noir Reader* (New York: Limelight, 1996), p. 205.

32 *Monthly Film Bulletin*, April 1950.

33 *The Sunday Times*, 18 June 1950.

34 *Sunday Pictorial*, 18 June 1950.

35 *Star*, 16 June 1950.

36 *News of the World*, 18 June 1950.

37 *The Sunday Times*, 18 June 1950.

38 Steve Chibnall and Robert Murphy, 'Parole Overdue: Releasing the British Crime Film into the Critical Community', in Chibnall and Murphy (eds), *British Crime Cinema*, p. 8.

39 Pulleine, 'Spin a Dark Web', p. 34.

40 *New York Times*, 10 June 1950.

41 *Variety*, 24 May 1950.

42 Ibid.

43 J. A. Place and L. S. Peterson, 'Some Visual Motifs of Film Noir', *Film Comment*, vol. 10 no.1 (January–February 1974), pp. 30–5.

44 Ibid., p. 34.

45 Ibid., p. 33.

46 Georges Sadoul, *Dictionary of Films*, trans. Peter Morris (Berkeley: University of California Press, 1972), p. 234.

47 Ibid., p. 244.

48 *Arts*, 15 December 1954; quoted in Wheeler Winston Dixon, *The Early Film Criticism of François Truffaut* (Bloomington: Indiana University Press, 1993), p. 133.

49 Ibid.

50 *Cahiers du cinéma*, no. 46, April 1955.

51 Ibid.

52 Quoted in François Truffaut, *The Films in My Life* (New York: Simon & Schuster, 1978), p. 209.

53 Ibid.

54 Ibid.

55 Raymond Borde and Etienne Chaumeton, *A Panorama of American Film Noir*, trans. Paul Hammond (San Francisco: City Lights, 2002), p. 5.

56 Ibid., p. 92.

57 Ibid., p. 93.

58 *Sight & Sound*, winter 1957/8.

59 *The Independent*, 2 April 2008.

60 *Guardian*, 27 March 2008.

61 *Guardian*, 6 December 2000.

62 *Guardian*, 2 August 2002.

63 *Village Voice*, 15 May 2001.

64 <www.dvdtalk.com/dvdsavant/s1493city.html>.

65 Ibid.

66 Edward Dmytryk, *Odd Man Out* (Carbondale: Southern Illinois University Press, 1996), p. 198.

67 Alain Silver and Elizabeth Ward (eds), *Film Noir: An Encyclopaedic Reference to the American Style* (Woodstock, NY: Overlook Press, 1988), p. 201.

68 Andrew Spicer, 'Introduction', in Spicer (ed.), *European Film Noir* (Manchester: Manchester University Press, 2007), p. 16.

69 Robert Murphy, 'British Film Noir', in Spicer, *European Film Noir*, p. 97.

70 Phil Hardy (ed.), *BFI Companion to Crime* (London: BFI, 1997), p. 242.

71 *Time and Tide*, 24 June 1950.

72 *Cahiers du cinéma*, no. 46, April 1955.

73 Filmed interview, *Night and the City* DVD.

74 Ibid.

75 Colin McArthur, *Underworld USA* (New York: Viking, 1972), p. 98.

76 Foster Hirsch, *The Dark Side of the Screen: Film Noir* (Aurora, CO: Oak Tree, 1981), p. 128.

77 Robert Warshow, *The Gangster as Tragic Hero in the Immediate Experience* (Garden City, NY: Doubleday, 1964), p. 131.

78 Ibid.

79 Paul Arthur, Essay, *Night and the City* Criterion DVD (2005).

80 Charlotte Brunsdon, *London in Cinema* (London: BFI, 2007), p. 25.

81 Arthur, Criterion DVD essay.

82 Erickson, 'Expressionist Doom in Night and the City', p. 205.

83 Nicholas Christopher, *Somewhere in the Night* (New York: Free Press, 1997), p. 77.

84 Brunsdon, *London in Cinema*, p. 101.

85 James Thomson, *City of Dreadful Night* (Whitefish, MT: Kessinger, 2004), p. 5.

86 Charles Dickens, *The Uncommercial Traveller* (London: Chapman, 1868), p. 150.

87 Ibid., p. 156.

88 Thomas de Quincey, *Confessions of an English Opium Eater* (London: Penguin, 2003), p. 31.

89 Stephen Graham, *London Nights* (London: Bodley Head, 1929), p. 87.

90 Thomas Burke, *English Night-Life* (London: Batsford, 1941), p. 38.

91 Gerald Kersh, *Night and the City* (Brainiac Books, 1993), p. 23.

92 Ibid., p. 3.

93 Patrick Hamilton, *The Midnight Bell*, in *Twenty Thousand Streets under the Sky* (London: Vintage, 2004), p. 49.

94 James Curtis, *The Gilt Kid* (London: London Books, 2007), p. 19.

95 John Worby, *Autobiography of a Spiv* (London: Dent, 1937), p. 32.

96 Chibnall and Murphy, 'Parole Overdue', p. 7.

97 Peter Wollen, *Paris Hollywood* (London: Verso, 2002), p. 137.

98 Ibid.

99 Robert Murphy, *Realism and Tinsel* (London: Routledge, 1989), p. 163.

100 Chibnall and Murphy, 'Parole Overdue', p. 8.

101 Frank Norman, *Stand on Me* (London: Secker & Warburg, 1959), p. 40.

102 Pulleine, 'Spin a Dark Web', p. 34.

103 Spicer, *Film Noir*, p. 180.

104 Steve Chibnall, *Quota Quickies: The Birth of the British 'B' Film* (London: BFI, 2007), p. 93.

Credits

Night and the City
USA/Great Britain 1950

US version

Directed by
Jules Dassin
Produced by
Samuel G. Engel
Screenplay by
Jo Eisinger
based on the novel by
Gerald Kersh
Director of
Photography
Max Greene
Film Editors
Nick De Maggio
Sidney Stone
Art Director
C. P. Norman
Music
Franz Waxman

©1950. Twentieth
Century-Fox Film
Corporation
Production Companies
Twentieth Century-Fox
presents
Produced by Twentieth
Century-Fox Productions
Limited
Produced and Released
by Twentieth Century-
Fox Film Corporation

Costumes for Miss
Tierney Designed by
Oleg Cassini
Costumes for Miss
Withers Designed by
Margaret Furse
Orchestration
Edward Powell
Sound Recordists
Peter Handford
Roger Heman

CAST
Richard Widmark
Harry Fabian
Gene Tierney
Mary Bristol
Googie Withers
Helen Nosseross
Hugh Marlowe
Adam Dunn
Francis L. Sullivan
Phil Nosseross
Herbert Lom
Kristo
Stanislaus Zbyszko
Gregorius
Mike Mazurki
'The Strangler'
Charles Farrell
Mickey Beer
Ada Reeve
Molly
Ken Richmond
Nikolas

US theatrical release by
Twentieth Century-Fox
Film Corporation on
9 June 1950 (New York).
Running time:
94 minutes 51 seconds/
8,537 feet.

UK version

Directed by
Jules Dassin
Produced by
Samuel G. Engel
Screenplay by
Jo Eisinger
based on the novel by
Gerald Kersh
Director of
Photography
Max Greene
Film Editor
Sidney Stone
Art Director
C. P. Norman
Music Composed by
Benjamin Frankel

©1950. Twentieth
Century-Fox Film
Corporation
Production Companies
Twentieth Century-Fox
presents
Produced by Twentieth
Century-Fox Film
Productions Limited
Released through
Twentieth Century-Fox
Film Corporation

Production Manager
R. [Ronald] Kinnoch
Personal Assistants to the Producer
Freddie Fox
Robert E. Dearing
Assistant Directors
George Mills
Percy Hermes
Camera Operator
Austin Dempster
Costumes for Miss Tierney Designed by
Oleg Cassini
Costumes for Miss Withers Designed by
Margaret Furse
Musical Director
Muir Mathieson
Sound Recordist
Peter Handford
Sound Editor
Esmond Seal

uncredited
Executive Production
Darryl F. Zanuck
Associate Producer
Otto Lang
Assistant Production Manager
Albert Pearl
Unit Manager
Percy Hermes
Production Secretary
Noreen Hipwell
2nd Assistant Directors
John Street
Douglas Hermes
3rd Assistant Director
Jack Green

2nd Unit Assistant Director
Anthony Hearne
Continuity
Peggy McClafferty
Assistant Continuity
Hazel Swift
Casting
Weston Drury Jr
Casting Assistants
Peggy Smith
John Jones
2nd Unit Director of Photography
Jo Jago
2nd Unit Camera Operator
Hal Britten
Focus Puller
Godfrey Godar
2nd Unit Focus Puller
Walter Lassally
Clapper Loader
David Oxenham
2nd Unit Clapper Loader
Eddie Earp
Grip
Joe Vincent
2nd Grips
V. Butler
A. Southall
Stills
Arthur Evans
Draughtsmen
Edward 'Ted' Clements
Peter Murton
George Beech
Wardrobe Supervisor
Ivy Baker

Wardrobe Master
Arthur Newman
Wardrobe Mistress
Evelyn Gibbs
Wardrobe Assistant
Len Hubbard
Make-up
Dave Aylott
Assistant Make-up
Eric Allwright
Hairstyling
Barbara Ritchie
Iris Tilley
Orchestration
Eric Rogers
Bernard Mayers
Cyril J. Mockridge
Sound Camera Operator
John Streeter
Sound Maintenance
Charles Van De Goor
Sound Floor Assistant
Hugh Strain
2nd Floor Assistant
Kevin Sutton
Boom Operator
William Cook
Wrestling Technical Advisers
Mike Mazurki
Micky Wood
Wrestling Trainer/Adviser
Walter Magnee
Publicity Director
Ernest Betts
Unit Publicity Representative
Arthur Allighan

Singing Voice Double for Gene Tierney
Maudie Edwards
Soundtrack
'Here's to Champagne' music and lyrics by Noel Gay

CAST
Richard Widmark
Harry Fabian
Gene Tierney
Mary Bristol
Googie Withers
Helen Nosseross
Hugh Marlowe
Adam Dunn
Francis L. Sullivan
Phil Nosseross
Herbert Lom
Kristo
Mike Mazurki
'The Strangler'
Stanley Zbyszko
Gregorius
Charles Farrell
Mickey Beer
Ada Reeve
Molly
Ken Richmond
Nikolas

uncredited
James Hayter
Figler
Tony Sympson
Cozen
Maureen Delaney
Anna O'Leary
Thomas Gallagher
Bagrag

Gibb McLaughlin
Googin
Aubrey Dexter
Fergus Chilk
Russell Westwood
Yosh
Derek Blomfield
young policeman
Edward Chapman
Hoskins
Brian Weske
messenger boy
Frank Pettitt
cabby
Hamilton Keene
bartender
C. Denier Warren
small American
MacDonald Parke
Eddy Reed
Americans
Ray St Bernard
The Strangler's opponent
Lew Marco
referee
Walter Magnee
a second
George Hirste
John Mann
Alan Tilvern
Leonard Sharp
beggars
Chunky Pattison
dwarf
Clifford Buckton
Clifford Cobbe
policemen
Charles Paton
watchman
J. Hubert Leslie
nightwatchman

Johnnie Schofield
cashier
Rex Garner
waiter
Peter Butterworth
Arthur Lovegrove
thugs
Freddie Watts
Stanley Escane
Philip Ray
John Sharp
John Rudling

Produced from 13 July–late October 1949 on multiple locations in London (Shot Tower, Cumberland Hotel,Victoria Station, London Bridge, Battersea Gas Holder, Piccadilly Circus, Glasshouse Street, White City, Hyde Park Corner, Ministry of Health – Whitehall, Anchor Pub – Bankside, Sports Garden – Strand, Waterloo Bridge, Howley Terrace, Exhibition Site, Bow Church, Figlers – Houndsditch, Mile End Arena, Irving Statue, St Andrew's Church – Queen Victoria Street, Café Anglais, Bagrags – Wentworth Street, Middlesex Street, King's Hall – Elephant and Castle, George Pub – Keyworth Street, Goodwin Court,

St Martin's Lane, Trafalgar Square, Jermyn Street, Strand, Hanging Sword Alley, Cobbs Court, Daily Mail Passage, Ireland Yard, St Paul's Churchyard, Piccadilly, Haymarket, Hammersmith Broadway, Cricklewood, Hammersmith Bridge, Lower Mall, Great Windmill Street, Denman Street, Richmond Buildings, Dean Street, St Giles High Street, Helen's Club, Mall Road – Hammersmith, Shaftesbury Avenue, Regent Street, Pheasantry Club, County Hall and Lambeth Bridge) including two weeks at London Film Studios, Shepperton, England.
35mm; black and white; mono – Western Electric Recording; 1.37:1; MPAA: 14096.

UK theatrical release by 20th Century-Fox Film Co. Ltd on 16 June 1950. Certificate: A (no cuts). Running time: 100 minutes 26 seconds/ 9,039 feet.

Compiled by Julian Grainger